Cows and Catastrophes

The Flights and Fancies of a
Cornish Dairy Farmer

T0347188

Cows and Catastrophes

The Flights and Fancies of a Cornish Dairy Farmer

Brindley Hosken

Old Pond PUBLISHING

A catalogue record for this book is available from the British Library

Illustrations by Rory Walker

ISBN 978-1-910456-48-4

Fox Chapel Publishers International Ltd.
20-22 Wenlock Rd.
London N1 7GU, U.K.

www.oldpond.com

We are always looking for talented authors. To submit an idea,
please send a brief inquiry to acquisitions@foxchapelpublishing.com.

Printed in the USA

Contents

Dedication

This book is dedicated to two women: my mother, Grace Hosken, and my wife, Ruth Hosken.

My mother, despite facing many difficulties in her life, always retained a positive outlook on life and hopefully taught me to do the same.

My beautiful wife Ruth has given me love and support for the last thirty years and given me the time and space to decide for myself it was time for the cows to go "up the road".

Reflections on Meneage

1 Farming in Meneage

The first section in this book is a series of articles about my farming, my fantasies (the ones I can talk about!) and my reminisces of the area where I live. Meneage.

Where on earth is Meneage? It is not on any maps, there are no signposts pointing to it and most people would not be able to direct you to it. It is a place I have lived all my life, on four different farms: Chywoone, Treveador, Trewothack and Withan.

Meneage consists of the parishes of St Martin, Manaccan, St Anthony and parts of the parishes of Mawgan and St Keverne. It means Land of the Monks and it is set on the southern side of the Helford River on the Lizard Peninsula in Cornwall. Meneage is in an Area of Outstanding Natural Beauty. Because of this and the picturesque villages nearby, such as Helford, Cagwith and Coverack, and the draw of the Helford River for boat lovers, it attracts people from all over the country who wish to live there or have a second home there.

Whereas the farming population is fairly static, with the majority of the farms in Meneage being owned and farmed by the same families for over fifty years, and in some cases more than one hundred years, the rest of the population is largely transient, with many moving down following retirement, but finding that Meneage is a long way from the rest of the country and their families, if illness becomes an issue.

The area itself has probably the mildest climate in Great Britain and we can go some winters with no frosts. This means that grass is growing for the majority of the year. The area also has a daffodil farm based there, that I work on during busy times. The majority of the farms are stock based but the soil is quite capable of growing good arable crops, including maize and winter cauliflower, or broccoli as it is known here. Unfortunately, because the area is on a peninsula, with water within three miles on three sides, fungal diseases are a problem for arable crops due to the sea mists and humidity.

My own farm is in St Martin parish and runs down to Frenchman's Creek on the Helford river. Frenchman's Creek is a local beauty spot made famous by the book by Daphne du Maurier. For those of you who have not read it, it is the story of a French smuggler and the lady of the manor. For those of you with no interest in literature (as if!), Frenchman's Creek is a local beauty spot made famous by Kylie Minogue filming her video for the song 'Flower', in which she leans languidly against a tree, wearing a long white nightdress.

I must confess that I have watched the video more often than I have read the book!

That reminds me: my fantasies, my what ifs?

What if *I'm a Celebrity* was set on a farm?

What if a tractor could write letters to a car?

What if Kylie came for tea? No, *no*, not that one!

What if there was a self-help group called Dairy Farmers Anonymous?

Read on!

2 Mick

At Withan, we have sixteen fields, with a footpath running through six of them. The footpath used to go through our garden and then down through the farmyard. About twenty years ago, I gently eased it to the left a bit! I know, I know, but it made it better for everyone. For the walkers, it made the path easier to follow and avoided them walking through the farmyard, where there were sometimes tractors working. They travelled through a small copse and came back onto the original path one hundred yards farther on. For myself, it avoided me being crept up on while I was in a corner closely inspecting the ivy. It was also safer when I was driving the loader tractor around the yard. A win-win situation for all concerned.

During the time the path went through our garden, we had a collie called Mick. Mick took exception to anyone carrying a bag. Any walker who had a rucksack on, he would target: he would jump up and bite the bag and try to pull it off them. The post lady was terrified of him, with good reason. My Grandpa told her, "If you want friends, you must be friendly." I think it would have been better if he had told the dog the same thing.

Mick also had a penchant for mud flaps. He would hang around any cars in the yard. He was not interested when they were stationary, but when they started moving, he was after them, grabbing hold of the mud flap and skidding all the way up the lane or until the mud flap came off. We had a collection of about thirty at one time.

Thankfully, when my brother got married and moved away, Mick went with him. No more abject apologies to irate car drivers. Or hidden smirks!

Not wanting to be without a dog, we found Patch, another collie. There was no vice in Patch. He was a lovely, friendly dog. He made friends with everybody. We would often get a phone call, "Your dog followed us to Helford and he won't go home." I would drive down to Helford and find him, whereupon I would be told, "He was looking hungry, so we fed him!"

"Of course he was looking hungry: HE … IS … A … DOG! And if he keeps coming down to Helford, I will have him shot!"

Needless to say, this did not go down very well. Patch never grew out of his wanderlust and during the summer he would often visit two pubs in the district to see what he could scrounge.

Did I have him shot?

Of course not, but one day he disappeared, and although the children missed him, I can't say I was that sorry.

3 Letter 1

Dear Car,

I realise that our relationship has been going downhill recently, since I took up moving daffodil bulbs from Manaccan to Constantine. I thought I should write this letter to try and clear the air. I know you think my annoying habits are sheer bloodymindedness, but in all fairness I cannot go any faster than 25 mph, and between Double Lodges and Garras there is absolutely nowhere to pull in. I know that pulling out of Gweek, I am down to less than 10 mph, but that is a consequence of having 11 tonnes of bulbs on the back. Finally, I know that when going around a left-hand bend, I am in the middle of the road, but this is only to stop the trailer from pulling stones out of the hedge and puncturing a tyre. For these grievances, I am very sorry.

On the other side of the coin, I feel I must point out some of your irritating little ways. The first one is when you play Tractor Roulette. This is when you overtake a tractor on a blind bend, e.g. Chygarkye corners. I suppose in Russian Roulette, the odds of getting seriously hurt are six to one. In Tractor Roulette, I would estimate the odds at about twenty to one. So far you have been lucky, but if your luck ever runs out, it will be "goodnight, Irene". Another of your annoying tricks is to drive through a wide part of the road and then stop at a narrow part and wait for me to squeeze through. Finally, when you are following me, is it necessary to get so close that I cannot see you in my mirrors? Contrary to popular belief, sometimes I do reverse and it is worrying if there is something behind that I cannot see.

I hope this letter has cleared the air and we can resume our previous amicable relationship.

Yours affectionately,

Tractor

4 Letter 2

Dear Tractor,

You have got a nerve! You do not understand me at
all! In fact, you have never understood me. You knew
I had MOT when you sent me that letter. As long as
you have got a big trailer behind you and your orange
light flashing, you think everything is all right. Another
thing: what did you mean by giving me mud flaps for
Christmas? What are you trying to say?

And my irritating ways: you make me stall, sanctimonious prat, lumbering up the road, expecting everyone to reverse for you, flashing your shiny red bonnet at anyone who looks twice at you, and mixing with those two idiots, John Deere and New Holland.

Tractor Roulette? You are the one playing Roulette, sending me a letter like that. You make me boil.

It's time for you to sharpen up, clean up your tyres and stop muddying up the roads.

I hope THIS letter has cleared the air!

Car

5 Cattle, Pigs and Sheep

It might be sad, but I like dairy heifers and I think, by and large, they quite like me. We have our moments sometimes, but that is natural in any relationship. When I look at them over a gate there is usually one that will come up to have her ears scratched and have a playful chew of my arm. They can annoy me by not going into the cattle crush. I usually crouch down, with a length of blue alkathene pipe in my hand (20 mm is my preference: I am more of an epee man than colichemarde!), and face them sideways, looking like a rabid crab, ready to move left or right with equal dexterity in a quite fetching scuttling movement. Most of the time, I am successful and can manage on my own. It's all part of the challenge.

My brother has half a dozen pigs. I quite like pigs. When you look over the gate at them, they usually come up, grunting contentedly, and they seem to enjoy having their bristly backs scratched. Are they pleased to see me because they think they are going to be fed pig nuts or other delicacies? No, I am sure they are not that fickle. They just like me.

During the winter, we have 130 sheep brought in to eat off any surplus grass, so that the grass grows fresh in the spring. I don't like sheep. They look at you with their vacant eyes and you know there is nothing going on in their tiny minds. Instead of walking through a gateway, they would sooner line up behind a small gap in the hedge and walk over in single file and make a bigger gap. If, when I go to check them, there is a sheep on its back with its feet waving in the air, I pull her back onto her feet. Is she ever grateful? Does she stay to have her ears scratched? Not likely. She is off, as if being chased by the Four Horsemen of the Apocalypse. It makes me feel quite unloved.

Not that I am desperate for friends, but it does get a bit wearing after a while.

I feel better having got that off my chest.

6 My Little Problem

I have got this little problem. I don't really like talking about it. When I go to a farmers' meeting there are a group of them laughing in the corner. How do they know? I am sure it is me they are laughing at. Is it the way I am walking? Am I mincing? Me and my little aberration. It is not impacting on the rest of my life yet, but for how long? I might as well stand at the front of the meeting and come out: "I can't weld, I can't weld, I just can't weld! There are worse crimes!" The humiliation, the sleepless nights, the dreams of the perfect seam, but I know I am only fooling myself.

I decide to go into the toolhouse and have another try. I slink in, put two bits of metal in the vice and switch on the welder.

The sweat is running into my eyes, my throat is dry and my hands are shaking as I try to strike an arc. See, I know all the right terms.

Tap tap phut.

Tap tap phut.

I adjust the amps.

Tap tap phut.

Tap tap phut.

I switch the other thing over.

Tap tap phut.

Tap tap phut.

Tap tap tap tap tap tap TAP phut.

I throw down the rod thing in frustration. Perhaps it's the welder: it is thirty years old. Yes, that must be it. I will buy a new one. A 350 amp mig one, with a gas bottle and copper wire and stuff.

I go outside feeling a bit better and my brother turns up. "Could you do a bit of welding for me?" I ask, sounding like Alan Carr.

He goes into the toolhouse, picks up the rod thing and FJJJJJJJ JJJJJJJJJJJJJJJJJJJJJJJJJJJJJJJJJJJT. He then picks up the chipping hammer, gives it a tap and the slag peels off in one long strip, revealing a pristine, even, bright, silver seam of magnificence, holding the metal together as if it will never let it go.

"Thanks," I squeak.

He gets back in his pickup, strokes his beard and rides off into the sunset. What a man!

Will I ever be able to do it? Or am I destined to have as my epitaph,

HERE LIES BRINDLEY HOSKEN

TAP TAP PHUT!

7 A Precaution

One of my favourite sayings at the moment is, "A precaution is never wasted!" I am always saying it to my children and anyone else who cares to listen. A couple of examples are filling up the car with fuel *before* the light comes on, so avoiding running out of fuel driving along Culdrose. Or spending thirty seconds shutting a gate when moving heifers, so avoiding spending an hour chasing them around a field.

If only I took note of my own wisdom.

We have two gates held together by a strap and a spring clip. The clip was getting a bit weak but I thought it would be alright so I did not replace it. The heifers started nuzzling it and managed to get it undone. They then went walkabout, all seventy-five in that batch, up the lane at one o'clock in the morning. Never a civilised hour. I didn't hear a thing, slept right through it. Symptom of an untroubled conscience, I suppose. Thankfully Ruth heard them and woke me. We went out and managed to get them back in, with only three of them getting in the garden and stanking the place up (treading the ground into holes with their feet). We were very lucky, as they had been to the end of the lane and could have gone anywhere, but instead decided to come back down the lane.

All was well in the end, just an hour of sleep wasted.

So remember. A PRECAUTION IS NEVER WASTED!

8 Letter 3

Dear Car,

Thank you for your letter, although you took so long replying, I thought I had done something wrong. Does sanctimonious mean stacked? You know your mate Push Bike? He held me up for ages the other day. I am just slightly quicker than him and it takes me ages to overtake. If you see him, could you ask him if he could just slow down a bit, just for a second or two when I am behind, so I can overtake him quickly, instead of being on the other side of the road for half a mile? I hate vehicles that inconvenience other road users!

By the way, do you fancy going off for a dirty weekend? I have been asked to pull cars out of the car park at the Royal Cornwall Show. It sounds as if there will be mud up to my pick-up crook. I have not seen mud like that since I pulled daffodils out of Gilly Farm. I cannot wait.

Yours hopefully,

Tractor

9 Letter 4

Dear Tractor,

Thank you for the invitation!

You will have to do better than that. If you think I want to hang around for hours watching you pull out those floozies, with their tops down, batting their headlights at you, you can think again. Why don't you ask L200? It sounds like more her thing. I hear she is well into mud, and with her four-wheel-drive, she might even do some pulling herself, if you get my drift.

I gave Push Bike your message. He said, I think it was, "Why doesn't he take off his beacon and shove it up his silencer, get off the road, park himself in the shed and service himself." Or something like that. I told him not to be so rude. He would not like it if you spoke to him like that.

Your friend,

Car

10 Burning Stubble

Twenty years ago, my brother and I used to enjoy doing something that is now illegal. No, not that! Burning corn arishes. After combining the barley, we would inspect the stubble, wondering if it would burn, then decide to give it a go anyway. We would rotavate the ditch to create a firebreak, and then with hearts beating fast, gather a bit of loose straw and catch it alight. If the stubble was clean with no weeds and the weather was dry, the fire would catch and the stubble would crackle furiously as the fire swept through it. It was at this point we would start to panic and wonder if our firebreak was wide enough. Racing ahead and stepping out the flames as they tried to leap our barrier, all around us the smoke would billow up, stinging our eyes and the heat would hit us like a blast furnace. Eventually the fire would die out, and with a bit of luck, we were left with a totally black field, all the weed seeds burnt to a cinder. The one problem about burning an arish, is that if there is a lot of green weeds in the bottom and it really needs burning, then it won't catch, and if it is a really clean arish and does not really need burning, it will burn like a dream.

The next job was to plough the field, and the furrows would turn over beautifully with the skims turning the ash under the soil and a small cloud of soot billowing up from each one.

We were left with a smile on our blackened faces and the satisfaction of a job well done.

11 Rotavating at Tregarne

One early morning last spring I went to rotavate a field at Tregarne. This field is the other side of the road to Roscruge Beacon and has amazing views over Falmouth Bay and the south coast of Cornwall. On this particular day, as it was a warm morning, a mist had formed over the bay and all that could be seen above the mist was Pendennis Castle. (I was once again left wondering why I never have a camera with me at all times.) All the modern houses and hotels along the front at Falmouth had been obliterated from view, along with the docks. St Mawes also had disappeared.

It came to my mind that in the mist, this was what my great-grandfather John Hosken would have seen, when he moved to Treleague to farm in the early 1900s, barely a mile away. Did he ever walk up to the Beacon to admire the view? Did any of his ten children? The view would have been the same as when the castle was built in the 1500s, when Henry VIII was on the throne, and although in the last five hundred years everything has changed, in some ways nothing has changed. I am still working the land, albeit with a 140-horsepower tractor, with a heater when it is cold and air conditioning when it is hot, rather than following a horse, with a hessian sack around my shoulders and subject to all the vagaries of the weather. I am still producing food from the Lizard Peninsula, as was my great-grandfather before me, and I assume generations of farmers before that. The same problems: sick animals, diseased crops, the weather, politicians. The same joys: healthy families, good crops, the sun on your back and the view from Roscruge Beacon.

12 Parc Tonkin

Some twenty years ago, one May day, we were carrying silage from the Parc Tonkin at Trewothack. Back and forth across the field, the tractor and forage harvester picked up the thick ranks of lush grass that had been mown down the previous day and blew the grass into the several trailers that were travelling back and forth from the field to the yard, where another tractor and buckrake were pushing the silage up into the clamp for the dairy cows' winter feed.

The beauty of this field is that you have a marvellous view of the south coastline of Cornwall and Devon, with Falmouth just across the bay and then further on St Mawes, Veryan, Dodman Point and in the hazy far distance, Prawle Point. On this particular day, the sun was shining and there were around a hundred boats of varying descriptions motoring, water skiing or sailing around the bay. In the late afternoon, the day cooled down and mist began to form on the water. It gradually thickened until it filled the bay and then made its insidious progress up the Helford river. At Rosemullion Head, the cliffs tried to halt its progress but the mist rolled up over the cliff like a giant roulade, unstoppable.

This now made an amazing sight, with perfect visibility across the bay to the clay pits at St Austell, but the only thing to see in the bay itself were the tops of the yachts' masts, just peeping through the top of the mist like little periscopes, a surreal sight and one I have never forgotten.

13　Royal Show

During the late '70s and early '80s, I had the privilege of representing Cornwall Young Farmers Club at tug-of-war for six consecutive years. Five years as part of Helston and St Keverne YFC and once as part of a mixed county team. For five of those six years, we reached the finals, which were held at the Royal Show at Stoneleigh, Warwickshire. I am proud to say that we came runners up in 1979 and we won the competition in 1980 (just thought I would slip that in).

The Royal Show was massive in those days. There were four entrances with a large balloon flying over each one. We used to come into entrance four. This would take us past a large river. The flood plain was filled at the time with huge irrigators, all working, and was totally alien to a young farmer from the deepest reaches of Cornwall. The show itself covered every sphere of agriculture that you could think of. There was an area devoted to wood processing, and large sheds full of every breed of cattle you could imagine, with the semen companies nearby. The Massey Ferguson factory was nearby at Coventry and every model of tractor and combine they produced was on show. Other machinery manufacturers were also well represented, displaying huge ploughs and other tillage machinery. The banks all had a permanent presence at the show, as did JCB and the National YFC, as well as various other agricultural institutions.

Besides an international pavilion for overseas visitors to relax in, and a dairy herd and a pig unit based on the showground, which was used for experiments and information, there was a large main ring with various attractions, among them the final of the YFC tug-of-war competition. In the tractor-pulling area, the more smoke the tractor poured out, the better the crowd liked it. No talk of carbon emissions back then.

We would leave the show buzzing, proud to be part of such a vibrant industry.

The last time Ruth and I visited the show was in 2003. What a disappointment! Half of the showground was empty. Of the other half, one third was devoted to agriculture, one third to horses and the final third to various stalls selling anything and everything. What on earth had happened?

Was it political?

M.A.F.F had become D.E.F.R.A., so there was no longer a Minister of Agriculture. Maybe agriculture and food was no longer deemed to be important. Was that a factor in the show's demise?

Or was it bad management?

Maybe the successful shows that are going from strength to strength, such as the Royal Highland Show, the Royal Welsh Show, the Royal Yorkshire Show and the Royal Cornwall Show, have all kept agriculture at their heart. Perhaps the Royal Show tried to be all things to all men.

It is a crying shame that such a show was allowed to just fizzle out, after being the huge showcase for the British agricultural industry that it used to be.

I am only grateful that I was able to visit the show in the years from 1977 to 1983 when the show was at its zenith and probably, dare I say, when I was at my zenith as well.

14 Harvest Fair

When I was in my late teens, the best day of the year in my opinion was Helston Harvest Fair. After spending all summer – when as I recall it never rained – combining, augering corn, baling and carrying straw (small bales), and with the harvest finished and twenty pound pay in our pockets, my brother and myself would load a couple of calves into the back of our mini pickup to sell at market and set off for Helston. We would realise it was a special day when starting down Grange Road and finding pickups and lorries queuing all the way to the market. Eventually after unloading the calves, we would head straight for "The Farmers Friend", a large stall that sold every thing a young farmer could desire, from donkey jackets to riding whips and from army-surplus raincoats to working boots with heel irons (essential for tug-of-war). To make it even better, the owner, Mr Phillips, would be standing at the front of the stall and selling whatever came to hand, with a slightly risqué story to help sell each item.

After seeing the calves sold and having a good look around, we would go home and milk the cows. Then back to the fair in the evening, a ride on the dodgems and maybe the big wheel and then back through the market as it was coming in dark, where Mr Phillips would still be selling and telling his stories. We would go home with our new donkey jackets, thinking it had been a very good day.

So, what about now?

The mini pickup has gone around land (scrapped).

Grange Road is now a cul de sac.

Helston Market is now a skateboard park.

Cows & Catastrophes

Harvest Fair is a shadow of its former self.

And even worse, Brindley Hosken is no longer in his late teens, or his late twenties, or his late thirties, or even his late forties.

And that is what they call progress!

15 Higher Poleo

My Grandpa Jenkin and aunty used to live at Higher Poleo Farm, near Blackrock, until 1976. Although it was only about fifteen miles from the more verdant climes of the area around the Helford river where we lived, it felt a world away. Grandpa had a TVO T20 and whenever I get a sniff of a TVO tractor nowadays, it takes me back to that time. Outside the house at Poleo was a long barn on your left, and as you walked past the barn, the whole vista opened up and there was a marvellous view towards the north cliffs and down over St Ives. Some winter evenings we would be at Poleo, huddling around the fire, while the wind howled around the house, sounding like a rabid werewolf looking for a way in.

One weekend my brother and myself were staying at Poleo and on the Sunday morning we got dressed in our finery and Grandpa took us both to chapel, but unfortunately he did not have the foresight to separate us, and so during the service we started playing up and being stupid. In the end it resulted in Grandpa having to take us home.

So what happened next, bearing in mind that he had five children of his own? Did he give us a strict talking to? No. Did he give us a smack on the behind? No. Did he send us to bed with no dinner? No. None of the above! Not to be outdone, he took us back to Poleo, sat us down and read to us from the Bible for the rest of the hour.

Lesson learned!

16 Letter 5

Dear Car,

I took L200 as you suggested, but I still had an awful time last weekend. I got stuck and everyone was laughing at me. You were right about John Deere. He is an idiot. He has gone and got two flashing beacons and they were flashing in time. He was show tractoring, pulling wheelies and spinning donuts. The worst of it is that L200 went off with him. They were chasing each other around while I was being pulled out. It was so humiliating. On the way home, I had a puncture and they both overtook me and did not stop to see if I was alright.

I know I am 4.5 tonnes and have a 3-tonne lifting capacity and a 200-litre tank, but I am a thenthetive guy, you know. Sometimes I need a hug.

I am not too worried about L200, she was not really my type, but I wanted to take somebody, for once. I wish I had not bothered. I suppose I am destined to be alone.

Yours sadly,

Tractor

17 Letter 6

Dear Tractor,

That was a bit mean of L200, after you went to the trouble of taking her to Royal Cornwall. I've always heard she is a little bit flighty. Never mind, one day you will look back on it and laugh. It is not a big problem in the grand scheme of things.

Unfortunately, I have to go to France in February to have my emissions sorted out, which is a bit worrying. It's just that my engine type, 2-litre TDI GT, is prone to the problem and they need to check it out, in case it gets worse. Why France? Goodness knows. I could really do with someone coming with me, for support. I don't suppose you can think of anyone?

All the best for now.

Yours expectantly,

Car

18 Language

I have a confession to make. Sometimes I use foul and profane language. It is not something that I am proud of, but sometimes cattle drive me to distraction. My mother, on the other hand, has to be extremely annoyed even to say "Shiiii…ugar". I believe she has sworn once in the last ten years. It must have been bad, because she has never told us which word she used, but I have got my suspicions!

I have tried to sugar the words up as well. As in, "Come on, my sweet, into the crush, in you go, cush, cush, NO, not that

Language

way, NOT THAT WAY, you stupid baaaa…sket case. No, don't jump the gate. DON'T JUMP THE GATE. DON'T JUMP THE FFFF… GATE. What part of 'don't' can't you understand, you bluuu…ssoming buuuu…tterball?"

It does not work for me.

I have therefore decided that my New Year's resolution will be not to swear any more. I am quite determined. In fact, I am feeling calmer just deciding that. I will turn on Smooooth Radio and may even get into a yoga position (don't do that, Brin, it will take them a week to untangle you).

What's that?

The heifers are out and running up the lane?

Shit!

And two of them are in the slurry pit?

Bleddy hell!

Get your sodding boots on and let's go!

19 Ploughing at Bosahan

Several years ago, one Saturday, I went to plough Helford Turn field at Bosahan. This field was a nasty field to plough, being fairly steep, and at the bottom very steep, with the Helford river just below. I started ploughing, and whereas in a normal field, at the end of each bout I would reverse and turn the plough over as I was going, drop it in the ground and on with the next bout, in this field, I would stop at the bottom, lift the plough just clear of the ground, turn it over and then gingerly turn the tractor around, looking at the water sparkling below my left shoulder, hoping that gravity did not take charge and send me sliding down hill and into the river. (It would have upset the boating fraternity.)

When half the field was ploughed, I stopped at the top of the field and had dinner. This gave me a view of all the boats moored on the river and across the river to Helford Passage and Durgan. I wondered why all those people were in their boats enjoying themselves, while I was busy working.

After dinner, I restarted ploughing and as the day wore on and the field turned from green to brown, a couple of buzzards turned up to look for worms and other delicacies; another bout and two more buzzards. During the day, more and more buzzards turned up. By the time I had finished the field, there were twenty-six buzzards following the plough. A record for me and a bonus on top of a good day's work. Better than sailing? For me, it was!

20 New Forage Harvester

Sod's law: "If anything can go wrong, it will!"

Murphy's law: "Sod was an optimist!"

During April 1987, we took delivery of a new forage harvester. It was duck-egg blue and scarlet, a Reco Mengele 25. A very smart-looking bit of kit. We bought it with my uncle, who we did silage with. While it was new, we had to take it from Withan to Trewothack. Unfortunately, it was a bit wider than our old forage harvester and got stuck on the bridge below Manaccan. While we were there trying to free it without damaging it, a lady came down from Manaccan and started bemoaning the slight damage to the bridge. Outwardly, I told her that we would not hurt the bridge and we would be very careful not to scratch the stonework or plaster. Inwardly, I told her to get lost and that I did not care if the whole bridge fell into the stream. Thankfully, we got it free after a bit, with just a few scratches on the side.

Now, there is a thing called a top link. It is about two and a half feet long, with an adjustable screw thread at each end to shorten or lengthen it. It is used to hitch implements to tractors and is made of metal. When you have a trailed mower, as we did, you do not need a top link. We would therefore tuck it behind the number plate, where it rode quite happily.

Some of you will know where this is going, but I will carry on anyway!

While mowing the silage on this particular day, the top link decided to jump off the tractor and bury itself in a rank of grass. Later on that day, the forage harvester entered the field and started picking up the grass. Unfortunately, the forage harvester did not have a metal detector fitted. It picked up the top link, and to be fair to the machine, it had a good stab at chopping up the top link. It managed to take off three chunks before bowing to the inevitable and shaking itself to pieces.

The damage was immense. All the blades were broken, the fly wheel was bent, the bearings were broken and the feed rollers were bent.

Why?

Why, when we had a new harvester?

Why not when we had the old machine?

Why could we not have picked up a bit of plastic, instead?

The forager had to go back and be practically rebuilt, more than a week's work.

I should probably have been on tranquillisers!

21 Tregithew

Before my youngest daughter started school, our daily routine included going to see the heifers at Tregithew. We would drive across the valley, walk out across the hills, count the heifers and make sure they all had "four legs and a tail". Then it was back in the car, drive on past Kestle, down Orchard Lane into Helford, have a look at the boats and then back home. This only feels like yesterday, but surprisingly she has now passed her driving test. This is what is known as quality time and I would not have missed it for anything.

I always hoped the heifers were at the top of the field, because it was hard work walking to the bottom and then back up again. From these hills was probably the best view of Frenchman's Creek you would ever get and a marvellous view across the Helford river to Calamansack.

Sometimes, if I went on my own, I would see three fox cubs gambolling together at the bottom of the hill. A slight noise and they were gone into the brambles, not to be seen again.

In the evening I would say to my children, "Do you want to come with me and maybe see some baby foxes?"

"Ooooh, yes please."

"You will have to keep very quiet."

"Alright."

I would load them up in the car and drive over to Tregithew, where they would all get out and shut the car doors very quietly. Then with the youngest one on my shoulders and the other two holding my hand we would stealthily walk out across the hill.

"I WONDER IF WE'LL SEE ANY FOXES, DAD," one of them would always shout.

"Um, no."

22 Letter 7

Dear Car,

You will never guess what happened. L200 dumped John Deere and went off with New Holland. Laugh? I nearly oiled my hydraulics. Serve him right. I saw him moping along the road the other day. I overtook him and managed to spatter mud all over him. Not that I am a vindictive tractor, but since that day, I have started feeling better.

I had a close one the other day: I was steaming along Nine Maidens with 2,500 gallons of slurry behind, heading towards Helston. There was a soft top (soft is right) coming from a road on the right. She waited and waited and then pulled out at the last minute. I slammed on my anchors, slewed around and the slurry tanker jack-knifed. Any closer to her and she could have had a paternity claim on me! Shook me up big time, I can tell you.

Sorry to hear about your emissions. It's not something you want to discuss with everyone, is it? I have been thinking about your other problem: what about asking Freda Lander to go to France with you? She is quite a sympathetic sort, very down to earth and good company.

Yours sympathetically,

Tractor

23 Letter 8

Dear Tractor,

That was a frightening story about the soft top. However, I do not like it when you are crude! Paternity claim, indeed. Any more like that and I will be an ex tractor fan!

I have always heard that you are a pretty dense tractor. Just how dense are you? I will try again. I could really do with some support when I go to France. I don't really want to ask Freda, as she is always so busy. Is there anyone else you can think of? I hear the Paris Agricultural Show is on while I am over there. That show is supposed to be the best in Europe. All shiny machinery and satellite navigation. I think it would be your sort of thing.

Yours hopefully,

Car

24 Frenchman's Creek

The last day of September and the mist has hung around all morning. After dinner it clears and turns into a beautiful day without a cloud in the sky. I walk down to see the in-calf heifers, across the roadway field, over the stile, down across the long hill and into the creek field. They are all there basking in the sun, and Tiny, the largest heifer, comes up to have her ears scratched. I duly oblige and she wanders off, content with the human contact, swishing her tail at the flies. Two choices: shall I walk back home or go down creek? Make the most of it, Brin, it will soon be winter. I hop over the gate, down through the path in the woods, to the creek. Take a look at the ash tree where my father carved his initials. BH 1955. That ash tree is a wisht-looking specimen, still only has a thirty-inch-girth – too much shade, I suppose. The grass of the quay is still a bit damp, but I sit down regardless. (You'll get piles, you silly boy.)

Frenchman's Creek!

Is it special because of the book, or is it special in spite of the book?

I sit there for several minutes savouring the silence. There is a slight hum from the insects in the trees, and in the distance a curlew calls and I get a snatch of conversation from two walkers on the path. Some of the trees on the banks have already shed their leaves and the others are starting to change colour, from greens to yellows and then on towards brown, preparing themselves for the winter to come.

I notice how the quay has eroded over the years. We were going to rebuild it when we had the time and the money, but unfortunately are still waiting for both. My mind drifts back forty-five years. We took a trip in the boat one evening, my father, my uncle, my brother and myself. Floss was left on the quay barking, but she decided to jump in and swim after the boat, so we pulled her in and she came as well. Out to the end of the creek and then out towards the mouth of the river, fishing with brightly coloured feathers for mackerel. Near the mouth, coming across the rubber boon stretched out from bank to bank, trying to stop the oil from the Torrey Canyon coming in and desecrating the river, and then back home, getting out of the boat, stiff with the cold. Forty years ago, walking down creek one fine April day and deciding to have a swim, no trunks, swam in my pants, dried in my vest and then walked home, chafing in all the wrong places. Thirty-five years ago coming down to the creek field to dig up horse thistles with a pick, and then, when finished, hot and sweating, going down for a swim. With my trunks, this time. With age comes experience.

The tide is coming in by now and I can see the grey mullet swimming lazily along, just below the surface. We could never catch them, even tried shooting them on one occasion. Never ever caught even one. My mind drifts back twenty-five years. Coming home from the Ferryboat Inn one night, my brother, my sister, my wife and myself, walking up the path in the pitch dark, holding hands so as not to lose the way, tripping over a tree stump and going down like a row of dominoes and then laughing until we cried. Ten years ago, taking my children down creek with a raft they had built out of four five-gallon drums and a pallet. Surprisingly it worked, and they had a very good evening, getting wet and starting their own memories of the place.

Five years ago and not such a happy memory. A gentleman decided that Frenchman's Creek was the right place to take his own life with a cocktail of whisky and sleeping pills. Thankfully, he was found in time and we carried him semi comatose, up through the woods to a waiting ambulance, thanking God that my problems had never seemed so big that suicide was the only option.

I wish that pontoon from Helford was not parked in the middle of the creek for the winter: it spoils the ambience of the place to a man of my sensibilities.

My mind drifts back to last Christmas Day. I went outside at four o'clock to check the sheep and went down creek afterwards. It was bitterly cold, the tide was out, and sheets of ice were lying on the mud flats, waiting for the tide to come in and float them off again.

My mind comes back to the present as I feel the damp seeping through my jeans, so I get to my feet and, having had my fix, head back home refreshed.

25 Milling

While my brother and I were at secondary school, Saturday mornings were set aside for rolling barley to feed the cows for the following week. The roller mill was a large cast-iron affair with two rotating steel rollers that could be tightened together to crush the grain. It was driven by a long, endless belt that was attached to a pulley fixed to the back of the tractor. Grandpa would stay in the mill house adjusting the rollers and shovelling the crushed grain into a pile at the back of the mill house. Chris and I were sent up in the barn and our job was to keep a pile of grain over the small hole directly over the mill. Being about eleven or twelve years old at the time, there were several things that we would rather have been doing. So we would pile up a large heap of grain and then sneak inside to watch *Banana Splits* on television. If we judged it right, we would get back in the barn just as the last bit of grain was disappearing down the hole and we could shovel up another pile without Grandpa being any the wiser. We would know if we timed it wrong, because he would come inside and point out the error of our ways in no uncertain terms. "One boy is a good boy! Two boys are half a boy! And three boys are no good at all!" The final statement would be used if we had a cousin with us.

Having to work every Saturday morning seemed hard at the time, but probably did us no harm. On a positive note, we did not have time to get into mischief.

26 Castlezens

Although I have lived in Meneage all of my life, I did once try to escape in the year 2000. I saw a farm advertised near Tregony. "TREGONY! That's thirty miles away! Are you gone mad! It's the other side of Truro!" Castlezens Farm was around 200 acres, with a modernised character farmhouse. It was run as a dairy farm but the farm buildings were in the main fairly antiquated. This seemed ideal: a nice house, fair stretch of land and a blank canvas for a dairy unit. The land was all touching, with decent-sized fields. You may wonder why we wanted to move? Withan is a hilly, difficult farm. It is land locked. It is water locked. It is too small for a reasonable dairy unit and it is in a corner (nobody puts Brindley in a corner). But it has two advantages. There is a picturesque farmhouse (Google Withan Farm Wing, if you want to take a look). It also runs down to Frenchman's Creek. These two things make it more valuable than it's worth as a working farm. We were hoping to double our acreage and go a fair way to erecting a dairy unit, if it all worked right.

Pretty obvious, really?

Our children, who were aged eleven, ten and seven at the time, did not see it like that and there were a lot of tears. We took them to look around the farm and the nearby beaches: "See, it isn't far, only an hour by car, nothing really." They were not convinced. This is when bribery reared its ugly head. Our youngest daughter, Frances, aged seven, stated that she would not move unless she could have a pony! Our son, David, aged ten, told us he would not move unless he had a quad bike! Our eldest daughter, Sarah, really put the kybosh on it by stating that she could not possibly move unless she had a new pair of flares to wear to school!

The summer was spent showing prospective buyers around Withan, while trying to negotiate the buying of Castlezens. A pretty stressful time. For a time, we thought it was going to happen, but in the end, Castlezens was sold to three different purchasers. A pity really, as we would have run it as a complete farm. However, we gave it our best shot and we have never regretted trying.

One positive thing: the children were pleased. By the way, Sarah may have got her flares, but the other two are still waiting.

27 Farm Safety

Monday 20 May 1968 was a bad day. We had gone off to school as usual. Me, nine years old , my brother Chris, eight, my sister Anne, six, my sister Jane, five. Our youngest sister, Mary, was a month old. When we got back to Trewothack in the afternoon, we were told that our dad had been killed in a tractor accident.

He had been out breaking in a hill when the tractor had overturned. He was thirty-six years old.

The next day, Chris and I walked out the lane, across the twenty-acres to the hill to have a look. The tractor, an International 434, was lying on its side with the silencer bent at right angles across the bonnet. Not a very big tractor, but big enough.

I suppose if the same thing happened today, a child would have a special bereavement councillor to help them through when they got back to school. In 1968 there was no such thing. We went back to school and tried to get on with it. Tried to find a strategy for coping.

At the time, I would quite often wake up in the night and be unable to get back to sleep. I would sometimes read most of the night. There was a marvellous view from our bedroom. By leaning out of my bed, I could look out of the window, out across Falmouth bay to St Anthony Head, where the lighthouse would be flashing, good weather or bad, come hell or high water. That lighthouse became my strategy for coping, it gave me a sense of permanence.

Did we lose out?

We boys never had our father patting us on the back and saying, "Good job done there, boys." Never had his advice when we needed it. Never had the chance to work with him on the farm. I think of the support that I have been able to give my daughters when they needed it and realise that my sisters never had that. Also my sisters never had their father there for the most important times of their lives, such as their wedding days.

On most farms there are things we know we should do. The slurry tanker with the broken PTO guard, the bull that is getting a bit cheeky, the trailer with the perished brake pipe. We will sort it out next week when we have a bit more time.

Have you got children or grandchildren ten years old or under?

I wonder how they would cope?

28 Trewothack

Trewothack Farm was a large farm for the area when my father and uncle bought it in 1967. They paid £36,000 for 180 acres, a large farmhouse, a farm cottage and a large courtyard of well-built traditional buildings. The first time I visited Trewothack, at the age of eight, I realised there were lanes to most of the fields and I thought how handy they were. In the next few months, my father had a large Atcost shed erected and put in a milking parlour. A 5/10 Weycroft Macford parlour, not very big by today's standards but quite modern for the time.

After my father's death, it became obvious that Trewothack was too big a farm for my mother to manage, with five children under ten to look after. So we moved to Withan and my uncle moved to Trewothack. We had a farm sale before leaving Trewothack and the four of us older children were running around, carrying papers from the field to the office and generally helping out. A local farmer told me thirty years later that he was at the sale and remembered us running around and thought how resilient children were and how quickly they get over things. I always regret not telling him that even though it was thirty years later, I had still not "got over things!"

We moved to Withan with twenty cows and my mother and grandfather farmed it, with help from my uncles, until Chris and I left school, some seven years later. My mother is a very strong-minded woman, who always looked for the positives in life and has hopefully taught me to do the same. It is only recently that I have thought how much of a struggle it must have been for my grandfather as well. He must have been about sixty-five when my father died, and he carried on milking cows into his seventies, to give Chris and me the chance to farm. We will always be grateful to both of them, for the sacrifices they made.

Ironically, my cousin, who now farms Trewothack, has planted the hill that my father was killed on, in trees for stewardship.

Different days!

29 Leaving School

I left school in 1975. I finished with no regrets on 20 June and bought a bottle of Corona on the way home to celebrate (I was always an innocent). Then home to our twenty cows: Anne, Jane and Mary, named after my sisters; Susan, Gillian and Mandy, named after my cousins; Kelly, Sabrina and Jill, named after Charlie's Angels. We also had Frances, Jessie, Gladys and Vera, Pixie (a kicker), Buttercup, a red and white Friesian, and Ermintrude, a cow with a bad turn in her eye who could not see very well, which did not help her temper. Finally, Amanda, Davinia, Elizabeth and Mildred. At the time, they were all tied up, fed hay and milked by three bucket units, with the milk being sent off in ten-gallon churns. I always wonder what on earth the bactoscan must have been in those days.

All the cows had their own individual stall, with their name written above. I would tell visitors that they could read their name and so knew where to go. All the cows were Friesian, apart from one, who was a Guernsey. She was the only cow to have horns. If she ever got loose, she would start butting the cow next to her, who would bellow loudly until help arrived.

At the time all the machinery we had was one tractor (a Massey Ferguson 135), a transport box and a scraper, but all things seemed possible in those days, with a bit of hard work and a bit of luck. Back then I did not have to worry about a lot of things, among them an overdraft, IACS, SFP, BSE, cross compliance, eartag inspections and milk quotas. TB tests were nothing more than an inconvenience.

In 1975 we had a good autumn and we were able to make a thousand small bales of hay in September. I can still remember the feel of those strings cutting into my hands. The usual Hosken way of making hay is to bale it up a day too early (just in case the weather turns) and then, when it starts bulging out of the shed, prop it up with telegraph poles!

Around the time Chris and I were leaving school, we were looking to expand cow numbers, and consequently all the cows were put to a dairy bull. Out of the twenty cows, eighteen of them had bull calves. Some people will tell you that things always even out. I would say that in thirty-five years of dairy farming, I never ever had ninety per cent dairy heifer calves.

30 Tractors

While visiting the Royal Cornwall Show last week, we came across a Massey Ferguson 135. This was the same make and model that we had when I left school, which is around forty years ago. Unfortunately, it was in the vintage section and I wonder what that is saying about me.

Our current tractor is a Massey Ferguson 5470, 140 horsepower compared to the 135's 47 horsepower.

The 135 did all our work at the time. It ploughed, spread dung and even pulled the silage trailer. In the winter, we would dress up in donkey jackets and leather gauntlets to try and keep warm. Although our 135 did have a cab, it was still bitterly cold. We would tuck a radio under the canvas of the cab, with an earpiece tucked into our ear defenders and listen to Tony Blackburn and Johnnie Walker on Radio 1. Nowadays, in the 5470, there is a radio built into the cab and I listen to Tony Blackburn and Johnnie Walker on Radio 2. Oh, how things have moved on!

Looking back and comparing, farming was a lot more physical forty years ago. We would have 20 tonnes of fertiliser delivered in June. All in 1 cwt bags (that's 50 kilos to you young uns). This would be unloaded by hand and stacked up. It would then be handled again when it was spread. Cows' cake would also arrive in bags and all have to be manhandled. Nowadays, fertiliser arrives in half-tonne bags and we can unload it with the tractor in no time. Cows' cake arrives in bulk and is blown into the barn.

It is the same with straw bales: forty years ago, working with my uncles, we would carry around ten thousand small bales of straw, all pitched onto a trailer by hand and then unloaded again in the yard. Hard physical work, blisters, callouses and shoulder aches. Nowadays there are big round bales of straw all carried by tractor and the most likely place to have aches and pain is in your behind.

Thank goodness for talcum powder!

31 Marijuana

Several years ago, I was at the Royal Cornwall Show. It was a hot, bright day and I had forgotten my hat. I looked around on various stands and came across a nice royal blue peaked cap with a brightly coloured emblem across the front. I bought it, and it kept the sun out of my eyes. Ideal.

Later on that day, we met my nephew, grinning all over his face. "Nice hat, Uncle Brin."

"Yes, I quite like it, I bought it earlier on."

"You know that is a symbol for a cannabis plant on the front of it?"

"Ooops."

Marijuana

For a while, I was in with the "in" crowd.

I was known by the younger generation as "Brinders with his cinders"!

32 Driving

I have a confession to make! I know I should not do it! I try to resist the temptation! But sometimes it gets the better of me and even though I know it is wrong, I sometimes succumb, weak man that I am. You must have guessed by now.

Sometimesidrivethetractorontheroad!

I drive up the lane, high up in the cab, looking over the hedges, farming all the land around in my head. It was a bit wet when they fertilised that winter corn, but it is a bit greener than the corn the other side of the road. Those bullocks are really stepping up that field. They will be out if they are not moved soon. That broccoli field has certainly caught the frost, you can smell it from in the cab.

Soon we have driven over the bridges and through Mawgan and are bouncing along Culdrose. I look in the mirror and see six cars behind me, I am going flat out, 25 mph and there is nowhere to pull in. It is about this time that I get a funny feeling between my shoulder blades, and I have worked out what it is: hatred! Unfortunately, some road users think that the only reason I am on the road is to cock up their day and to make them late for their next appointment. I have always tried to drive with the thought that it is better to be ten minutes late in this world than twenty years early in the next. However, some drivers do not seem to agree with that philosophy and when they see a tractor they seem to lose all road sense and have to pass it, whether it is safe or not. This has resulted in the past by my being overtaken by a bus on a blind left-hand corner and being overtaken by an articulated lorry on a 100-yard straight bit of road.

Driving

The only time that I do not pull in while driving across Culdrose is during the summer holidays, because if I did, I would not get out again until September.

I hope this has given you some insight into the other side of things, and if I have ever held any of you up, I sincerely apologise and would say that I am not a bad bloke really, and am certainly not any of those things you called me at the time.

33 Harvest Festival

When I was young, one Sunday evening my grandparents took me to the Harvest Festival at Rosuic chapel. I remember the faint hiss and flickering yellow glow of the gas lights (how old am I?). Ever since then I have loved Harvest Festival. Whether this is because the service is a validation of what I do, what my father did and what both my grandfathers did, in that we ploughed the fields and scattered and we gathered in the grain, and we saw the bright robes of gold the fields adorned.

My own favourite harvest hymn is no longer in the Methodist hymn book, but the first verse is as follows:

> *Now the year is crowned with blessing*
> *As we gather in the grain;*
> *And, our grateful thanks expressing,*
> *Loud we raise a joyous strain.*
> *Bygone days of toil and sadness*
> *Cannot now our peace destroy;*
> *For the hills are clothed with gladness,*
> *And the valleys shout for joy.*

Nowadays, I suppose, the majority of the population would not attend a Harvest Festival service. I don't know whether this is because we live in a secular society and life is too busy, or because for the last sixty years food has been plentiful and the supermarket shelves are always full of food from all over the world and none of us can envisage a time when this might not be the case.

Either way, I will be at Meneage Methodist Church at Manaccan in October to celebrate the Harvest Festival.

34 Minor Procedure

I was used to performing minor procedures on our animals: dehorning, castrating, removing extra teats, etc. Six months after the birth of our youngest daughter, Frances, I went into hospital for my own minor procedure, a vasectomy.

A what?

A Vasectomy.

Oooooh!

We went up to Treliske hospital one morning. Ruth told me, "You'll be alright, just breathe away the pain. Phwa, Phwa, Phwa."

We went inside and I was given a hospital gown to put on. Now I am a fairly tall person (six feet three inches, in my prime). The hospital gown was fairly short. I had to stoop down and shuffle my feet to preserve my modesty. I need not have worried: fifteen minutes later, I was lying in an operating theatre, with a bank of a dozen floodlights lighting up my inadequacies. Bit of local anaesthetic, bit of prodding and pulling, bit of stitching and that was the end of my "minor procedure"!

I was then wheeled into the recovery room, where I fainted clean away. Ruth said it was because I was a wimp, but I know it was because I had had nothing to eat for fifteen hours.

We got home later in the day, and when I got out of the car, I had to stoop down and shuffle my feet so as not to snag my stitches.

The phone rang as we got inside. It was one of my cousins asking if I could help lay a load of concrete the next day. I declined, blaming a bad back.

After a few days, I was back on my feet, firing on two cylinders, and looking back, best day's work I ever did.

35 Propinquity

Many years ago in the distant mists of time, I read a book by John Cherrington called *On the Smell of an Oily Rag*. In that book I came across a word that I have been dying to use ever since. That word is propinquity, or more specifically, occupational propinquity. If you do not know what it means, you will have to look it up. Today is the day I am going to use it. So if you are ready, here goes.

My grandfather bought Withan farm in August 1953 for the sum of £5,000. What amuses me is that in the deeds, the agreement is between John Stanley Vyvyan (gentleman) of Trevalsoe, St Keverne and William James Hosken (farmer) of Boundis Farm, Mabe. Obviously my grandfather was not thought of as a gentleman.

Withan has a footpath running through it, and out of sixteen fields, the footpath runs through six of them. At the top side of the farm, the path runs from the farmyard across three fields to the next farm of Mudgeon, less than half a mile away, where the Jenkins' farmed. Obviously during the next few years that path got a lot of use, because in five years, Brian Hosken had married Grace Jenkin (my father and mother), Frances Hosken had married Kenneth Jenkin, and Mary Hosken had married Ronnie Jenkin.

The most unusual case of *occupational propinquity* that you are ever likely to come across. Three Hoskens from Withan marrying three Jenkinses from Mudgeon. This situation is extremely rare – even for Cornwall.

And NO, it does not make me inbred!

36 Letter 9

Dear Car,

Sorry I have taken so long to reply. Unfortunately, I was run into by a white van man. He hit me so hard that it nearly shook my front weights loose. It was on the road near my place – you know: narrow, greasy and full of bends. He then told me that he was *only* doing 40 mph, well within the legal limit. I wanted to reverse back and ram him, to try and shake some sense into him, but I am really not that kind of tractor. (I am a lover, not a fighter.)

Now, how dense am I? I am 4.5 tonnes of denseness and that is pretty dense, you know. And by the way, I have always wanted to go to the Paris Show.

Oooooooooooh!

I don't suppose, no, that is, well, um, I don't suppose you would like me to come to Paris with you? I have a bit of holiday to come and, well, you know? I would look after you during the emissions tests and we could look around a bit afterwards. How about it?

Yours in anticipation,

Tractor

37 Letter 10

Dear Tractor,

Now, why didn't I think of that? I would love for you to come and look after me. I will sort out the travel arrangements and headlight shaders. I might even try and shake your front weights loose myself when we get there!

You must try not to get into any more scrapes with white van men, or soft tops, or anyone else driving along the road. Try and keep your bonnet clean.

Ooh, I am really starting to look forward to it now. Paris, here we come.

Yours excitedly,

Car

38 I'm a Celebrity, Monday and Tuesday

Monday

Welcome to *I'm a Celebrity, Get off my Laaaaaaaaaand!*

The celebrity doing the farm tucker trial today is the American rapper, Fifty Pence. Good morning, Fifty, how are things in camp this morning? Good. Now our farm tucker trial this morning is called Cattle Crush Conundrum. As you can see, the cow is secured in the crush with a yoke locking her head. She can move her head, but cannot get out. Your challenge is to lift her head up and drench her with that bottle of medicine. Willing to give it a go? Good.

Yes, she does make it awkward by dropping her head right down on the ground. Yes, she is a bitch.

You got her! You got her, now get the drench in the corner of her mouth, quickly.

Oops! … Dr Bob, Dr Bob.

Tuesday

Welcome to *I'm a Celebrity, Get off my Laaaaaaaaaand!*

I am sorry to say that Fifty Pence left the camp yesterday on medical grounds. Unfortunately, while taking part in the trial yesterday, the cow raised her head with such force, she smashed his hand against the crush and he is in hospital having treatment.

Never mind, the celebrity doing the trial today is Mary Celeste, the reality star from *COWIE*. Morning, Mary, how are things in camp this morning? Missing Fifty? Yes, pity about that. Our farm tucker trial today is called Placing the Placenta. As you can see, there is a cow in the crush. She calved over a week ago but had a retained afterbirth. The vet has been and removed it. Your trial is to pick up the placenta with a heavil (four-pronged fork) and carry it to the pit over there. As this is a farm tucker trial, you will find that the smell will be unbearable. Willing to give it a go? Great.

That's it, Mary, pick it up.

UUUUUUUUUUUUGH.

I think you've got it.

UUUUUUUUUUUUGH.

What does it smell like, Mary?

UUUUUUUUUUUUUUUUUUUUUUUUUGH.

Nearly there, Mary. Mind it doesn't slip.

UUUUUUUUUGH.

Careful, Mary, it is slipping, mind you don't step on it. DON'T STEP ON IT.

Oops! … Dr Bob, Dr Bob.

39 Canada

In the days when we were milking cows, we used a fair percentage of bull semen from Canada. During November 2004, we were offered the chance of going to Canada and visiting top herds of Canadian Holstein cattle. At that time, we had never been abroad and we had never flown. Our first flight, therefore, was Heathrow to Montreal. In for a penny, in for a pound.

Our group of four couples and two semen reps landed in Montreal after a six-and-a-half-hour flight, met our driver, Bob Schmidt, and headed off to the Hotel le Dauphin in Saint-Hyacinthe, which was our base for three nights. This town was in the Quebec territory.

Thursday 4 November, we set off for a full day of farm visits. Seven farms, with three of the farms being top herds. Deslacs, Comestar and Karona. At the time, we were using several bulls from Comestar, namely Comestar Outside, Comestar Leader and Comestar Lee. This made the visit particularly interesting to Ruth and me.

Friday 5 November, we visited one farm, Le Presentation, then in the afternoon visited the Quebec Red and White Holstein show, held at Saint-Hyacinthe. We also looked around the huge shopping mall in Saint-Hyacinthe. (You can have too much of a good thing.)

Saturday 6 November, another three farms: Limbra, Breeze Hill and Glengarry. Glengarry was the most interesting farm to me. It was farmed by Canadians who originated from Scotland. The area was practically a Scottish enclave and they even had their own Highland Games. After the farm visits, we headed to the Holiday Inn Hotel in Ottawa.

What surprised me most about the Quebec area was that even though Canada is bilingual, so many Canadians spoke French and could not understand a word of English, and, I suppose, vice versa.

Sunday 7 November. No cows today! We looked around Ottowa in the morning. Ottowa was a mixture of French and English speakers and it seemed incongruous to see a bronze statue of the Queen, sitting on a horse, by the Houses of Parliament. We also saw black squirrels in Ottowa. During the afternoon, we travelled from Ottowa to Gananoque, a town on the banks of Lake Ontario. During the evening, we watched an ice hockey game nearby. What a rough, brutal game.

We loved it!

Monday 8 November, another three farms: Ronbeth, Crovalley and Fricosons. The majority of the farms we visited in Canada managed their cows with the same set-up. The cows were tied by the neck and fed silage from a tower attached to the cows' house, thus negating the need for the farmer to go outside during the winter. (Interestingly, in Britain it is now illegal to tie animals by the neck.) Most of the tower silos we saw had the name of the farm written on them. Monday night, we stayed in a hotel in Peterborough. We were told that if we had been there the night before, we could have seen the Northern Lights! (Hey ho…)

Tuesday 9 November, we woke to a white world. Not enough to stop us, but just enough to look pretty. Three more farms: Randy Fish(!!), Lochmar and Sunny Maple. We also travelled through the Mennonite district near St Jacobs. We passed one farm where they were spreading dung (manure) and ploughing with horses. We followed a horse and carriage along the road. The school had hitching rails instead of car parking spaces and there were half a dozen horses tied outside the school. This area was within a mile of big industrial units. A fascinating way of life and I would like to have found out more. We stayed Tuesday night at a hotel in Kitchener.

Wednesday 10 November, seven farms today and a visit to a bull stud. The first farm was Summitholme. This was the first farm we had visited that was more like a British set-up, with 350 cows in a cubicle house, with a 24/24 rapid-exit parlour. A pretty impressive system. We had dinner at the bull stud, where we saw several famous bulls (well, I had heard of them): Silky Gibson, Lheros and Silky Cousteau. After visiting the other farms, we headed off to the Intercontinental Hotel in Toronto (or Tronto, as we who have been there like to call it).

Thursday 11 November. Had breakfast in the restaurant of the Intercontinental Hotel (as you do). Had dinner from a chip van outside the Intercontinental Hotel. After a tour around the city, we arrived at the CN Tower. We travelled to the first level, at 1122 feet high, where there is a restaurant and a glass floor. It is supposed to be elephant proof, but I was not sure if it was Brindley Hosken proof, so I did not stand on it. Just did not seem sensible. We then went up farther, up to the Sky Pod, 1465 feet high. What a view: the whole of Toronto and the vast expanse of Lake Ontario in front of us. In the afternoon, we visited the Royal Winter Fair. What a show. Twenty acres under cover, with competitions for every sphere of agriculture. The Cavalcade of Horses, the Celebration of the Dog, reindeers. Dairy cow competitions followed by the Sale of the Stars: some of the best heifers in Canada, up for auction. Competitions for all sorts of vegetables – half-ton pumpkins – and beautiful wheat sheaves. During the evening, we went to a reception at the show, sponsored by Semex, the company that arranged our trip.

Friday 12 November, Ruth and I had a walk around Toronto in the morning. Half of the city's shops were underground, because of the freezing cold temperatures in the winter. We ended up in Chinatown somehow. In the afternoon, we went back to the Winter Fair. We were told that on the Friday of the show, sixty thousand school children from all over Canada attend, to understand where their food comes from. What a terrific idea. In the evening we walked to the Royal York Hotel and had drinks with the boss of Semex, in his suite.

Saturday 13 November, our last day In Canada, we travelled to Niagara (that's another one off the bucket list). I expected Niagara Falls to be out in the wilderness, but no: if you turn around after looking at the Falls, there is an enormous hotel and casino. Very surreal. Wearing very fetching yellow capes, we travelled down behind the Falls to watch and hear the roar as the water tumbled past. We had a meal in the restaurant overlooking the Falls. I don't think I gave the waitress a big enough tip, as she came back and practically threw my credit card at me. Funny the things you remember. We left Niagara at five o'clock, travelled back to Toronto airport and caught the plane back to Heathrow. This trip took less time than the bus trip from Heathrow to Cornwall.

My impressions of Canadian farming were that the dairy industry had supply management in the form of milk quotas, and that the government were strong supporters of agriculture and were willing to protect the farmers from cheap imports. Many of the dairy farmers were milking around sixty cows in a tie-up cow shed that was up to eighty-five years old. They did not appear to be under financial pressure. In Great Britain at the time, the milk price had dropped around eight pence per litre from its highest point and this was causing great financial pressure. Most dairy farmers were expanding, to try and protect their income. The milk processors would cut the price and we would produce more milk. A recipe for disaster.

I also discovered that dairy farmers are the same the world over. Happy to show others around their farms, with a great pride in their livestock. Usually combined with a black sense of humour.

It was an honour to look around their farms and their country and to be made so welcome. It was a trip we will never forget.

40 Milk Stands

For several years after I left school, we sent our milk away in ten-gallon milk churns. In 1977 we bought a refrigerated bulk milk tank and gradually churns were phased out. By 1980, practically all milk was collected in bulk. Outside most dairy farms there was a milk stand. This was a level platform about four feet high, either free standing or built into a hedge. The full churns of milk were put onto the milk stand every day. The milk lorry would pull alongside and the full churns wheeled straight onto the lorry and empty churns left ready for the next day's milk.

Recently, I have been noticing that there are still a surprising number of milk stands still around. The best example I have seen is outside Lower Relowas, between Newtown and Double Lodges. There are also milkstands outside Tregonwell in Manaccan, at the entrance to Porky Street in St Martin and opposite the shop in Mawgan. There are also several in Gunwalloe.

I don't know whether this makes me an anorak, or whether I should get a life and take up trainspotting instead. I am sure someone will let me know.

41 I'm a Celebrity, Wednesday

Wednesday

Welcome to *I'm a Celebrity, Get off my Laaaaaaaaaand.*

I am sorry to say that Mary Celeste left the camp yesterday on medical grounds. Unfortunately she slipped on the placenta during the trial and dislocated her shoulder.

Anyway, the celebrity doing the farm tucker trial today is Glen Coe, the Winter Olympics bob sleigher. Morning, Glen, how are things in camp? A bit depressed?

Never mind, our farm tucker trial today is called Shivering Straw Pile. All you have to do is to find the five stars in the straw pile. Of course, as this is a farm tucker trial, the thing that makes the straw shiver is the critters, or more specifically rats. Look, you can see their scaly tails peeping through the straw. Willing to give it a go? Great. Rather you than me.

That's one star, well done, Glen, that's two stars, plenty of time. Is that blood? … Dr Bob, Dr Bob.

42 YFC Secretary

My daughter has just finished twelve months as secretary of Helston and St Keverne Young Farmers Club, some twenty-seven years after I spent twelve months as chairman of the same club. I was wondering what things had changed and what things have remained the same. The competitions have remained largely unchanged, with brains trust, debating and other speaking competitions still prevalent and various sports still contested. My own sport of tug-of-war has changed somewhat. When I pulled, the finals were held in July at the Royal Show in Stoneleigh. I had the privilege of pulling at the Royal Show for five years, reaching the final on two occasions and winning the title in 1980. The final was held in the main ring and I always thought it was an honour to pull there. Nowadays the finals are held in October, at a college in the Midlands, where I don't think it has the same kudos (might be my age).

When my daughter wanted to relay a message to all the members, she would send a text message with just one click (amazing, these newfangled ideas).

Frm wk th nt rby club 7 lol

What's lol?

Laugh Out Loud, Land Of Leather, Leaves On Line, Lots Of Love?

In my day there were no mobile phones. I had to ring the members up on their landline and sometimes, heaven forbid, speak to their parents first.

Nowadays, the chairman and secretary have to be CRB checked by the police before taking office. And the chairman now seems to have to take responsibility for all the club members, whereas I always thought that they should be responsible for their own actions.

Risk assessments need to be carried out before It's a Knockout. Fair enough, I suppose, as we had a member who hurt his neck badly by jumping into a pool of water during this game.

The Young Farmers county office also now has to have an Ofsted inspection, which was quite a surprise to me.

The main thing my daughter did different to me was to get engaged to her chairman halfway through the year.

LOL.

Make your own mind up!

43 Carol Service

Every year, Cornwall Young Farmers hold a carol service in Truro Cathedral. The cathedral holds approximately nine hundred people and is usually packed for the occasion. The nativity is quite special, with a real donkey carrying Mary to the stable and the shepherds turning up with live young lambs. Afterwards, there is a Christmas disco.

My own association with this service started when, at the age of fourteen, I was chairman of Helston School Young Farmers Club and was asked to read a lesson. I remember the lesson was Micah chapter five and started with "But thou, Bethlehem Ephratah!" A little bit worrying at the time. I attended the service many times as a member of Helston and St Keverne YFC, and still remember the pride I felt, as chairman, carrying the club banner to the front of the cathedral during the first hymn. One year, I left my headlights on and returned to the car after the service and the dance, only to find the car would not start. We had to phone my uncle at one in the morning to come and get us. He never said a word that night … He came down after I had milked the next morning and was at a very low ebb and pointed out the error of my ways!

Several years ago, our children had the chance to take part in the nativity, as two shepherds and an angel. This is unusual as they are usually all angels!

For many years recently, it has been necessary to apply for tickets to attend the service. Last Christmas, after being elected as President of Helston and St Keverne YFC, without having to ask I was sent an invitation to attend.

At the end of the service, looking back over forty years of being involved with YFC, I wondered if I should stand up and sing "The Circle of Life".

44 Flora Dance

I expect that most of you have heard of the "Floral Dance", the song that charted when Terry Wogan sang a version in 1978. Some of you may be happy to forget it. I have to confess that Flora Day and the Flora Dance is part of my heritage, as Helston has been my home town for all of my life and my great-grandfather, John Hedley Benney, was mayor of Helston, back in the mists of time.

At this stage, I have to admit that I have danced the Flora Dance not once or twice, but ten times.

Flora Day takes place on 8 May unless this date is on a Sunday or Monday, when it is held on the Saturday (Monday was market day). The town of Helston is decorated with bluebells and sycamore. There are four dances on Flora Day: the seven o'clock, the children's dance, the midday and the five o'clock dance. Plus the Hal-an-Tow, a pageant heralding in the spring with guest appearances by St George, St Michael, St Piran, dragons and Spaniards.

All of the dances are the same steps and all follow Helston town band through the streets of Helston, through the throngs of people who congregate to watch the festivities. The tune sounds fairly simple and it is only when the band passes by that you can hear the different nuances in the music, by the different sections of the band.

The seven o'clock dance starts at … guess. This dance is for mainly young people of the town and surrounding area. The men wear white shirts and grey trousers and a Flora Day tie. The girls wear short summer dresses, ideally in bright spring-like colours. In all of the dances, buttonholes of lily-of-the-valley are worn. I took part in this dance once, in 1976. All three of our children have taken part in the seven o'clock and will no doubt try to get an invitation to dance this year.

The children's dance starts around ten o'clock. The children from the four schools in Helston can take part. There will be over a thousand children dancing, all in white, the boys wearing their school ties and the girls wearing headdresses of flowers, representing their school colours. I have danced this dance five times, while a pupil at Penrose Road and Helston Comprehensive.

The midday dance is arguably the most important dance of the day. In this dance, the gentlemen wear morning suits and top hats and the ladies wear long dresses, big hats and gloves (and flat shoes, if they are sensible). The midday dance is about three miles long, moving through the streets, in and out of the shops. It can get extremely warm in a morning suit and I think pride must get some people through it. Ruth and I have danced the

46 I'm a Celebrity, Thursday and Friday

Thursday

Welcome to *I'm a Celebrity, Get off my Laaaaaaaaaand.*

I am sorry to tell you that Glen Coe had to leave the camp yesterday on medical grounds. Unfortunately, he was bitten by a rat during the trial and is now in hospital on an antibiotic drip.

I'm a Celebrity, Thursday and Friday

Never mind, the celebrity doing the farm tucker trial today is David Hosken, the fencing maestro. There is nothing he cannot do with a bit of barbed wire. Morning, David, how are things in camp this morning? A bit empty?

Ah well, the farm tucker trial this morning is called Slurry Surprise. As you can see, we have a slurry tanker with 1300 gallons of slurry on board. There is a small six-inch pipe on the back with a rubber cone on the end, bringing the outlet down to two inches. Unfortunately, there is a fodder beet blocking the outlet. Your task is to clear the fodder beet. Willing to give it a go? Jolly good.

David, David, you may want to release the pressure in the tanker before you start undoing that clip. DAVID, release the pressure first. DAVID … Too late!

Friday

Welcome to *I'm a Celebrity, Get off my Laaaaaaaaaand.*

Unfortunately David Hosken had to leave the camp yesterday because he stank so badly. He is apparently still in the bath.

There will be no King or Queen of the Farm this year because there is no one left. See you next year.

The farm tucker trials
CATTLE CRUSH CONUNDRUM

This happened to my sister-in-law, who crushed her finger quite badly in a cattle crush.

PLACING THE PLACENTA

I know of a farmer quite near to me who would leave a bucket of water for the vet and disappear to the other end of the farm if the vet was coming to remove an afterbirth, because of the smell. Stepping on it is equivalent to walking on ball bearings.

Shivering Straw Pile

I was bitten by a rat once, while injecting a cow that was lying on the ground. I did not see it, which was just as well, as I would have had the screaming hab dabs. I hate rats. It was only later that evening that my arm started itching. When I looked, I had two small bite marks in my arm and a three-inch red ring around it. A dose of Weil's Disease did not appeal, so I went straight to hospital and got a course of antibiotics.

Slurry Surprise

This has happened to David, my son, and also to me. Luckily David is the one with the photograph showing it!

47 Switzerland

During March 2008, I was given the chance to travel to Switzerland and look at the dairy cattle there. Now, I like a good cow as well as the next man, but what really interests me is the set-up of farms in different countries, the opportunities and difficulties the local farmers have and what drives them to farm the way they do.

On 28 March, I left home at two a.m., drove to Bristol airport, met the other six in the party and caught the plane to Geneva. Ninety minutes later, we were descending towards the bright blue of Lake Geneva, with the snow-covered Alps in the background. Spectacular. We picked up our hire car and headed off to a bull stud that was near Zurich, 150 miles away. At least we saw a lot of the country. At the bull stud, we were shown some of the top bulls in Switzerland. It was interesting that in Switzerland, we could observe the bulls with just a wire-netting fence between us. Whereas when we visited a bull stud in Canada, we were only allowed to see the bulls through a glass screen. This stopped us breathing our nasty English germs over their bulls.

Unfortunately, after leaving the bull stud, we had an accident with the hire car and wrote it off. This involved an unscheduled stop at a police station and took three hours. We left at six-thirty p.m., with 150 miles to travel to an international reception held in Bulle, in the Gruyère region. We were then treated to a Gruyère fondue meal. I don't want to be a Philistine, but it smelt of old socks. I tried a piece to be polite, but, after a twenty-hour day, I was feeling decidedly delicate and was glad to get back to our hotel.

Saturday 29 March, we visited the Black and White National Holstein Show, held in Bulle. An interesting point was that some of the cows had horns, something that you would not see in dairy competitions in the UK. When the champion cow had been chosen, a group of Swiss dairy maids came in with yokes on their shoulders. These yokes had cow bells hanging off them and made a fair old racket. The trophys that are presented in dairy cow competitions in Switzerland are not cups, as in England, but are cow bells of various sizes. We saw some that would not look out of place on an elephant. On Saturday afternoon, we visited another farm. The view from the farm was amazing. A green plateau and then in the distance, snow-covered mountains. This farm's altitude was 3000 feet above sea level, a bit different from Withan, where the altitude is from zero to 260 feet above sea level. All the farms we visited produced milk for Gruyère cheese. They were not allowed to feed silage, because Gruyère cheese is not pasteurised. Silage would have provided a risk of listeria. All the farmers, therefore, fed their cows on barn-dried hay. They pulled their milk to the factory in stainless steel milk tanks on wheels. Some were still using milk churns to transport their milk. During the evening, we drove around the area and got some idea of the scale of the mountains nearby.

Sunday 30 March, four of our group travelled back to the show to watch the Red and White Holstein Show. To me a good cow is a good cow, it does not matter what colour she is. Joe and I had a lie-in, had a leisurely breakfast and then looked around Charmey, the village we were staying in. We discovered a ski lift at the bottom of the village. During the afternoon, we travelled up the lift, taking us from 2600 feet at the village to 5200 feet at the top. It was the last official day of skiing in the area, but thankfully we did not have any gear.

Monday 1 April, Dominator Day. We visited seven farms to look at Dominator daughters. I know that for some people, that would be their idea of hell. Yet, I know some people who are willing to go to Truro and visit seven clothes shops, not just once, but every week (that's hell!). One of the farms we visited had recently constructed a new building. The cows and the farmer's family all lived in the same building. There was a massive space on the second storey, where they stored machinery. I only had one problem with it. The thought of rats. Uurgh. Another farm we visited was in a village. Outside, they had what most people would call a midden. I would call it a dung pile. I cannot imagine what would happen if I had a dung pile in the middle of our village. I would probably be put in the stocks. A third farm had a top herd of cows, milked through a robot. He also looked after bulls for a Swiss semen company. His trophy room contained around a hundred cow bells that he had won in various dairy competitions.

Tuesday 2 April, we travelled to Echalarns Farm. The farmer fed the cows by means of a large gantry crane in the roof of the building. It was just a matter of grabbing some barn-dried hay from one side of the shed, swinging it around and dropping it in front of the cows. Easy peasy. Finally it was back to the airport and home.

My impressions of the Swiss dairy industry were that there were around forty thousand dairy farmers in Switzerland, averaging twenty-five cows each. A number that would just not be economic in this country. As far as we could gather, they were receiving about double the milk price that we were. It would have been interesting to visit some of the herds that were grazed high up in the mountains, during the summer, to see their special problems and opportunities. Once again, finding that you are a fellow farmer negates most barriers.

48 Withan's Hills

Withan's hills are not the longest hills in the world, but there is no escape lane at the bottom, no level area. They go straight from hill to woods. The first time I spread fertiliser on them, I was petrified, bearing in mind what happened to my father. People tell me what a pretty valley it is. I tell them it would be a lot prettier if it was level! When I go on the hills to spread fertiliser, I always put dual wheels on the back, to make the tractor more stable, and I never drive on them unless the grass is dry. As you can imagine, this makes them very difficult to manage, especially in a wet year. During 2012, for example, I only managed to fertilise them once. They will also poach and step badly if we leave the heifers on them in wet weather. Several years ago, while spreading the hills, I drove over a patch that had water running over it. The tractor slipped and I tried to stop, but the tractor turned with its front wheels uphill and then it took off like a ski jumper. It slid to the bottom at an alarming rate, with myself unable to do anything about it and hoping there was not a tree waiting at the bottom, to stop me permanently. Thankfully it stopped about ten feet from the woods at the bottom of the field. It frightened the stuffing out of me and retaught me a valuable lesson. Don't take liberties.

Opposite Withan's hills are Tregithew hills. One day while turning hay (it was a long time ago), I noticed my neighbour starting to drive down the hill. I thought, if that was me, I would reverse down. I turned the corner and looked back. My old physics lessons came back to me. Potential energy and kinetic energy. The tractor was hounding down across the field with one of the back wheels spinning backwards. My neighbour had jumped out, thankfully.

We both made our way slowly to where the tractor was. It had reached the bottom on four wheels, surprisingly, and smashed into a tree. My neighbour was shaking and lit a cigarette to calm himself down. It was one of the two times in my life that I thought a cigarette sounded like a good idea! The other time was when our parish council were trying to get a new parish hall built and the bureaucracy we encountered nearly drove me to smoking.

No! Filthy habit!

49 Hercules

The following piece of writing contains material that those with a sensitive disposition may find disturbing. If you think this applies to you, I suggest you do not read it, but turn over the page. If, however, you do read it, don't come moaning to me afterwards!

There was a time when we had a Hereford bull at Withan. We will call him Hercules. Hercules was a busy boy. He was riding the cows with vigour and everything seemed fine. Unfortunately, the cows kept returning. We looked closer and found that Hercules was not "working" properly.

He was "covering the earth with good things".

He was "not reaching Shangri-La".

He was "sending his parcels to the wrong address".

It is no good, I will just have to be crude. Hercules had a bent penis! Unfortunately, it was not a problem that could be easily ironed out and Hercules had to be sent up the road. It was not his fault, but he made a heck of a mess of our calving pattern and cost us a lot of money in the short and longer term.

50 Combining

One August day some thirty summers ago, I was chosen to drive the combine for the day. I filled it up with diesel and drove out to the Griddle where a lovely crop of barley was waiting for me. I set the combine up and then dropped my eight-foot six-inch header into the crop and started combining. I was THE MAN. Soon I had combined several rounds of the field, and started back and forth across the field, leaving a golden rank of straw to mark my progress. As the morning wore on, the baler turned up and started baling the straw. As the knife cut through the crop and it was transported away, the dust rose up and with the heat of the sun on the back of my neck, I could feel the sweat trickling down my neck, creating white rivulets in my blackened face. Man, machine and nature as one.

I finished another strip and then weaved my way between the bales. Swinging the combine around to begin another strip, I heard an almighty BANG. I looked to my left where the unloading auger should have been, but it was not there: it was flopping against the combine side with a piece of cast iron dangling from it. I had caught it on a tree in the hedge.

I drove into the yard to give my uncles the good news, where my worth as a member of the human race was called into question. Eventually we got hold of our local blacksmith, John Pearce, and he came out and after a struggle managed to weld the cast iron back in place. I often wonder if the character assassination he heard that day was what drove him to change his vocation and come back as the Rev. John Pearce.

As for myself, I cannot remember if I was allowed back on the combine or was banished to shovel grain for the rest of the day as penance. I suspect it was the second option.

51 Hanging Gates

One of my favourite jobs on the farm is hanging gates. There are about thirty field gates on Withan and another twenty around the yard, so I have plenty of practice. When you are going to put up a new gate, the first thing you need is a hanging post. We usually use concrete posts that we make. We make up moulds and then fill them with concrete, then put the hangings in and finally scratch our names and the date into each post and allow to dry. The next step is to dig a hole for the post with a shovel and bar. We then put the post in and concrete around it and check that the hangings are vertical. When the concrete has dried, we hang the gate and then we can see where the latching post needs to go. We usually use a wood post for the latching post: this is because if you get it in the right place, you can drill a hole in it for the gate latch to slide into. When the latching post has been concreted in and gone hard, we hedge up around both posts and put some barbed wire across the new hedging to stop the cattle rubbing them, and that's job done. There is one gate at the entrance to the creek field that was made of an old hay rake. It is hung on a gatepost made in 1964 and I assume the gate was made at the same time by my uncle, Geoffrey Hosken. It is surprising that it has been hanging on the same post for over fifty years. I lengthened this gate some years ago. My part is less aesthetically pleasing. If any of you have walked the footpath between Mudgeon and Helford, you may have seen this gate.

One of my least favourite jobs is sorting out gates for a second time because someone has desecrated them. A large cow or heifer can trundle towards a gate and think, I am Red Rum and I can jump that gate. They're not and they can't. They usually get stuck on top and then wait for us to sort them out. This invariably leaves the gate with the top bar bent and the hangings crooked, looking a proper mess. Another way of ruining a gate is for some dope to catch the gate post with a trailer. This creates a lot of work, replacing the hanging post. The third way is when a gate swings shut as you are driving through it and you think, I will just give it a nudge with the tractor wheel. I must confess I have been guilty of this crime. Either the gate will swing open and break something, or it will snag in the tractor wheel and break something. Whichever way, it is not a habit to be encouraged.

Fifty years ago, gateways were about eight feet wide. Nowadays, if we were putting in a new gateway, we would probably put in a fifteen-foot gate.

52 Stewardship

At Withan, we are in a countryside stewardship scheme. This scheme pays us a certain amount of money for farming in a way that helps the environment. We have to amass a number of points to qualify, with various options available to us. Among the options are hedgerow management, planting wild flowers, wild bird seed mixture in grassland and buffer strips around fields. Buffer strips are left unplanted around the edges of fields, to act as wildlife corridors. They are more appropriate for large arable farms. We are in the entry-level scheme. There is a higher-level scheme, but this would seriously compromise our farming, if we took part. We struggle to amass enough points for the entry-level scheme.

Most of our points come from hedgerow management. We agree to trim our hedges only every other year instead of every year, which used to be our custom. This is supposed to make a better habitat for nesting birds.

In my opinion, at Withan sycamores will grow at eight to ten feet a year, and after two years we are struggling to trim trees of two to three inches' girth. This, I feel, leads to a less dense, more straggly hedge, and after two years our hedges are looking decidedly scruffy. I liken it to myself, instead of having a number four crewcut as usual, deciding to grow dreadlocks and a beard. It may be better for the wildlife, but I would certainly look a mess. However, rules are rules, and if I want the money, I have to abide by them.

The Dairy
Farming Years

53 Dairy Farming in Meneage

I was approached in late 2007 to see if I would be willing to write, as a regular contributor, articles about dairy farming locally, for the *Meneage Messenger*. The *Messenger* is a local magazine covering four parishes in the Meneage area. I agreed and this section of the book covers the time period from 2007 until the present day. Some of the articles are political, some are tongue in cheek, some contain a lot of financial detail, but all are appropriate to the time they were written and what I was thinking at the time.

I started writing with a pen and paper, then moved to the computer and a memory stick, finally discovering email.

Below is the first article that was published. It was the first thing I had written since leaving school some thirty-two years before! I have not altered it at all, so it is how it was written at the time.

> As I have agreed to write a regular contribution in the *Messenger*, I thought I had better start by telling you about our dairy farm. We farm at Withan, which is on the border between St Martin and Manaccan, and which runs down to Frenchman's Creek. Withan is about 120 acres and is quite a hilly farm. I also rent most of my brother's land at Lannarth Gate Farm, on the far side of Manaccan.
>
> Yes, I am the nuisance that has six or seven tractors and trailers driving up and down through Manaccan from early morning till late at night at various times of the year.
>
> At Withan, we have about 120 cows and about 60 youngstock. At the moment all the animals are inside and do not go out in the fields at all.

I thought it might be interesting for you to know what each cow eats in a day in the winter. 6.5 kgs protein blend, 0.5 kgs straw, 14 kgs fodder beet, 20 kgs grass silage and 22 kgs maize silage. That makes a total of 63 kgs/cow/day. In addition to this, our top yielding cows get up to another 6 kgs of cow cake in the milking parlour. If you multiply this by 100 cows, you will realise that they are eating over 6 tonnes of food a day. With this going in the front end, you can imagine what is coming out the back end.

2007 was the year that Tony Blair left No. 10 and it is interesting to note that when he became Prime Minister in 1997, the average price we received for our milk for the year was 23.2 p/litre. When Mr Blair left No. 10, ten years later, the average price we received for our milk was 15.3 p/litre. Quite a difference, I think you will agree.

During the past ten years over half the dairy farmers on the Lizard Peninsula have stopped producing milk. Most of us who are left have probably doubled our production in that time in an effort to stay in business. During the first half of 2007, we were wondering if there was any future for us in milking cows, as with the best will in the world, we could not produce milk for under 16p/litre and speaking to other dairy farmers it was clear that a lot of them were thinking the same thing.

In the second half of 2007, things started looking better with the price of milk being talked up instead of talked down, and there was a bit more optimism in the industry, instead of total despondency. In October, we had a substantial price rise and for the first time in ten years, things started looking better for our future as dairy farmers.

To get some comparison, the average price for milk at the moment in this area in April 2016 is less than 21p/litre, less than it was nearly twenty years ago in 1997.

54 Kicked

Whenever I showed visitors around my milking parlour, usually their first question was, "Do you ever get kicked?" The answer, surprisingly, was "Not very often." I was kicked in the leg once and knocked down into the shi**y straw. This was probably my own fault for not letting the cow know I was there. In the parlour I would occasionally get a whack on the arm, usually as a result of not concentrating on what I was doing. The cows that kicked every milking were not the problem, but the cows that were quiet for a fortnight and then lashed out with no warning were the frightening cows. It was not long before they were "up the road" (that's a euphemism for made into beefburgers). I did not worry about a little tap as long as I had a nice bruise to garner sympathy with. "That's not much of a bruise, I don't know what you are fussing about."

Kicked

The worst kick I ever had was not by a cow, but by a donkey. He was rolling in the dust and I gave him a poke with my boot. He got up and let fly with both barrels, catching me with them both. He then trotted off into the field. I swear he was laughing at me, not that I could see him: I was doubled over with my hands on my knees as wave after wave of pain washed through and over me. After fifteen minutes, I finally managed to straighten up and tottered down to the yard. Thankfully it did no permanent damage, but it was the closest thing I ever got to a do-it-yourself vasectomy.

55 Silage

Here at Withan Farm, we try and do our silage around 20 May. This is not the whole story. We try and spread four thousand gallons of cow slurry on the silage ground during January and February, weather permitting. This cuts down on the artificial fertiliser we need to spread and so saves us money. The next job is to roll the silage fields. If you do this right, you can make pretty light green and dark green patterns in the fields. We like to drive around the field three times one way and then turn around the other way three times, etc. Some farmers drive back and forth making stripes. Some farmers just keep going around one way. I feel that this shows a distinct lack of imagination.

The main aim of rolling is not to make pretty patterns, but to push any objects such as stones or bits of metal into the ground and out of harm's way, where they will not get picked up by the machinery. The modern forage harvester is over 500 horsepower. It can pick up a tonne of grass in a minute and chop it all to an inch long. You can imagine what would happen if there was a large stone in the grass. The man who owns the forage harvester is apt to get a teeny bit upset. Most modern harvesters have a metal detector fitted on the front that will stop the machine instantly before any damage can be done by a piece of metal. A small piece of wire an inch long will stop it. This would not be a problem to the machine but could prove a problem to the cow, if she ate it. Unfortunately a metal detector will not detect stones.

We usually try and put some artificial fertiliser on the fields in early March. I aim to get it done on 1 March, if possible. This is not essential, but gives me the impression I am in control. We give it a second dose in early April and then wait for the grass to grow.

The grass quality is at its best on 10 May, but 20 May suits us better, because the grass bulks up considerably during the middle of May. All we need is a day or two of good weather and no "isolated thundery showers" and we can bring the silage in, hopefully of good quality, good quantity and dry. Ready for the winter that is to come.

56 Freemartins

Sometimes cows have twins. This is fine if they are both female calves. However, if there is one calf of each sex, then the heifer calf will be infertile. These heifers are called freemartins. For some reason, I always want to refer to them as freemasons. *I try not to, as it would make me appear inarticulated.* Some of these freemartins are easy to spot, as their "bits" are not right and some of them will even urinate out sideways because of this. Some of them look normal on the outside and there is nothing to show that they are not right.

Some years ago, we bought some weaned heifer calves from Holland. There were ten of them in the bunch and they all looked alright. Unfortunately, when it came time to breed them we discovered that three of them were freemasons. This was very annoying, no less so when we discovered that other farmers in the district had been caught in the same way. One farmer nearby had fifty per cent freemartins in a group that he had bought.

I decided that, even though it might have been an innocent mistake, I was not going to buy any more Dutch bull semen, to teach them a lesson.

That'll learn 'em!

57 Stress

I was very sorry to hear the other day about the death of a local dairy farmer and I was even sorrier to hear that he had taken his own life. It made me start to think about the pressures of dairy farming. For me they were:

1. Financial pressure. Ongoing and relentless, and I assume, as this country is languishing near the bottom of the European price league, that there are many farmers feeling the same pressure.
2. Sick animals. Especially when their sickness called into question my stockmanship, as in calves with scour, spreading through the whole house and several dying. Or, if two cows did the splits in the yard on the same day.
3. Shooting healthy animals. In the past, there were times when there was no market for dairy-bred bull calves and the only option was to shoot them. Pulling them out of the house for the kennel man to shoot, I found incredibly stressful.
4. The weather. Not a big problem for most of the year, but at silage time, hearing the phrase "isolated thundery shower", would start my heart beating faster. In the past, I have cut all my silage down and then the heavens have opened. I have then sat in a chair and listened to the water running down the yard, as the adrenalin coursed through my veins.
5. Inspections. Dairy inspections were not a problem, but why the inspector always turned up just as I had washed the scraper tractor off outside the dairy door I do not know. Farm assurance inspections I could not abide, as I thought they were a complete waste of time. A paper exercise. Lastly, an eartag and paperwork inspection, especially when carried out by a patronising official who took two and a half days to

complete the job, when I was quite proud of my paperwork abilities.

I believe financial pressure is the most stressful because:

- Sick animals mean higher vet bills, means more financial pressure.
- Shooting healthy animals mean no money for them, means more financial pressure.
- Bad weather during silage time means poor-quality silage, means more cow concentrate, means more financial pressure.

Adding to these pressures is the problem that, as farmers, we cannot switch off at five o'clock on Friday afternoon and pick up again at nine o'clock on Monday morning, refreshed. A sick cow, for example, is there all weekend to be looked after and to remind us of our failings.

And if we were to go to the doctor suffering from stress and the doctor said, "Take a fortnight off and come and see me again," would it happen? Either we would carry on as before, or we would remain indoors, trying to relax and fretting even worse about what was happening outside.

On top of this is the fairly easy excuse we have to withdraw from any outside human contact, with a raft of plausible excuses for avoiding people, such as "I would love to come to your party, but I have a bunch of heifers calving," or "I really must get on top of this paperwork," or "I have got to get those grass seeds rolled in before the rain."

Finally, I would just like to say that I am quite a cheerful bloke really.

58 316

Back in May 2008, Withan Igniter Budock was one of my favourite cows, or as I liked to call her, 316. She was one of our best, on her third lactation and consistently milking over 45 litres of milk since calving on 3 November. On her second lactation, she gave 11,430 litres of milk at 3.68 butterfat and 2.93 protein with a somatic cell count of 14. Her quality was a bit low, but acceptable for the amount of milk she gave. She was also a good-type cow. If I had a hundred like her, I would have been quite happy.

Unfortunately 316 had to go to that great milking parlour in the sky, where the radio is always tuned to Radio 2. She had the dubious honour of being the first animal on this farm to go down with tuberculosis.

Every year, every animal on the farm over six weeks old has to be tested for TB. One of our vets comes and injects them twice on the side of the neck, and then comes back three days later to read the results. If the lower injection site has a bigger lump than the higher site, then she is a reactor. During 2008, we had five inconclusives, which as far as I can remember is the first we have ever had. Because they were inconclusive, they had to be tested again two months later, by a D.E.F.R.A. vet this time. Two of them were positive reactors: 316 and 211. They were then slaughtered. We got compensation for them at £1230 per cow, which may sound a lot of money, but I would reckon that to replace a cow like 316 at that time would probably have cost over £2000.

As we then had TB, we had movement restrictions placed on the farm. We were not allowed to sell anything unless it went straight to slaughter, which was not a problem at the time, but became so in the autumn, when we wished to move some stores (twelve-to-eighteen-month beef bullocks) and sell some calves.

You may think that we would not be tested again for another twelve months, but this was not the case. Because we had reactors, we were tested every sixty days until we had two clear tests. As you can imagine, it was not an easy task, bringing all the animals in and running them through the cattle crush, especially the six-month-old calves. Some farms, not many miles from here, have been under restrictions for many years and others have had half their herd go down at one time. I hoped and prayed that our outbreak was just a minor blip.

Where does TB come from? Our herd was pretty well closed, with the only animal brought in during that twelve months being a bull brought in to pleasure the cows. He was tested before arriving and again before departing. Every animal over six weeks old that is sold in the market and not going straight to slaughter has to be tested in the six weeks coming up to sale in this country, to try and stamp out TB, but as our experience shows, it was not working. We then come to the wildlife, or more specifically badgers.

Unfortunately, like it or not, badgers are part of the problem, and saying they are not is like saying the Black Death had nothing to do with rats (lovely furry creatures).

TB is a welfare issue for cattle, which is why they are tested every year and any reactors culled. Unfortunately it is also a welfare issue for badgers, and in this country the badger has no natural predators, so there is no friendly lion or tiger to dispatch any that are diseased or ill. This means that TB has to run its course, which, as it is predominantly a lung disease, results in weakness, coughing, loss of weight and finally open lesions on the throat and lungs. Not a nice way to go.

What were the answers, bearing in mind that there were 7232 farms under TB restrictions during 2008?

A TB vaccine? A nice idea, but still at least ten years away.

Carry on as we were, culling cattle and leaving the badgers in peace? Obviously not working, as our own case showed.

Finally, and no doubt very unpopularly, culling the cattle and culling the badgers where there were large outbreaks of TB. This was the option the Welsh Assembly took to deal with the problem of TB. I admired them for making a decision and not sitting on the fence, hoping the whole issue would go away, as our own Minister for D.E.F.R.A., Hilary Benn, was doing at the time. Surely all our aims should have been healthy cattle and healthy badgers?

On 5 July we had our sixty-day retest and unfortunately had another reactor, another third calver. Ironically, that was also the day that Mr Benn had come to a decision about TB: carry on doing nothing, taking out the cattle and leaving the badgers alone. A case of Nero fiddling while Rome burned.

Cows & Catastrophes

In autumn 2015, Parliament voted to start bombing Syria. Mr Benn, as Shadow Foreign Secretary, voted in favour. It amazes me that our MPs are quite willing to vote to bomb other countries and agree to all kinds of unpleasantries, but when it comes to making a decision on culling badgers and sorting the TB problem out once and for all, they come over all mealy mouthed and squeamish.

59 Factory Farming

Some time ago, I read that the Women's Institute were having a debate on factory farming at their AGM. I thought I would give you my thoughts on the subject.

To start with, the term "factory farming" is very emotive and almost guaranteed to raise the hackles of the mildest WI member. I assume the term means herds of cows that are housed for twenty-four hours a day for 365 days of the year. In this country, I would estimate approximately five per cent of the herds of dairy cows are indoors all of the time, approximately five per cent of herds of cows are out all of the time, with the remaining ninety per cent going in and out depending on the weather, the time of year and the ground conditions.

The main aims of herds outside all of the time are to take as much cost as possible out of the business, to rely as far as possible on grazed grass and to manage the herd as far as possible as one cow. This entails drying all the cows off in December (no Christmas Day milking), then starting calving in early February, with the aim of calving everything within eight to ten weeks, then starting serving the cows at the beginning of May, with the aim of getting them all in calf in as short a time as possible.

The advantage of this system are that the cows are working with nature, with the cows calving just as the grass starts growing and served when the days are getting to their longest. This helps their fertility. The other advantage is that there is very little money tied up in expensive buildings. Most herds on this system are relatively low output, with some of them only milking once a day. The disadvantages of this system are that a very wet spring can ruin their grassland, with the cows trampling down more grass than they eat. Also there is not the opportunity to rehouse them. This system of dairy farming is known as "extended grazing" or "the New Zealand system".

The main aim of herds inside all of the time is to maximise output and to feed the cows a consistent diet all year around. I have visited a herd of over a thousand cows on this system and I was very impressed with the management, the cleanliness and the welfare of the animals. This herd were in groups of around two hundred cows. I think it is probably easier to manage two hundred cows all at the same stage of lactation than one hundred cows at all different stages, with some freshly calved, some stale milkers and some due to dry off, all on the same basic ration. The cleanliness of this herd was achieved with a large flush of water that swept all of the slurry away and left the cubicle shed much cleaner than I could obtain by scraping with a tractor scraper twice a day. The cows in this herd are fed a TMR or total mixed ration, where all the concentrates the cow might need are mixed with the silage, which is better for the digestion of the cow. The cows have also got rubber mats to walk on, to and from the cubicles. The disadvantages of this system are the large capital outlay in tractors, feeder wagons and buildings and the fact you are trying to beat nature by calving cows all the year round.

Both of these systems need their own kind of cow. Most of the cows indoors all of the time would be pure Holsteins, with the ability to produce at least 10,000 litres in a lactation and weighing around 700 kilos. Most of the cows outside all the time are usually crossbred Jerseys and Friesians producing up to 5000 litres and weighing around 500 kilos.

If it was a choice between the two systems, I would have my cows indoors all the time, because I am soft hearted. When I used to go out last thing at night during January, with the rain beating off the roof and the wind whistling, I would look at all the cattle, lying down, chewing their cud, and think, thank goodness they are all indoors. I would not like the thought of my animals out in such weather.

60 Starlings

Sometimes when I go outside, there is a starling sitting on the lawn. It looks a plain bird at first sight, but when you look closer, you can see the iridescent shades of greens and purples among its plumage and the flecks of white on the tips of its feathers. Quite a beautiful bird really. It looks at me with its bright eyes and then flies away, clearly unimpressed.

Sometimes, when thousands and thousands of starlings get together, they put on a magnificent display of close formation flying called a murmuration (try Googling "starlings on Otmoor" for a spectacular video). They all fly in one vast swarm, creating intricate black and grey Spirograph patterns in the sky. One of nature's true spectacles. They then disappear into the distance.

I know where they go!

They fly to the nearest dairy farm and land in the surrounding trees, chattering excitedly like a bunch of five-year-olds at their first birthday party. The food has been put out for the cows, a lovely sweet mix of grass silage, maize silage, wheat and soya, worth maintenance plus twenty-five litres. Then down they swoop, thousands of them. You cannot see the silage because of the seething mass of starlings. They pick away at the maize grains, the wheat and the soya, dropping their ordure as they go. I shout at them, put my hand on the gate and feel the starling guano slide up between my fingers. They fly away, leaving a soiled mess of silage behind, with that unmistakable smell. They have not gone far. Their next port of call is the maize clamp: they land on the face and eat the maize grains and pull the rest out, dropping it on the floor. By the next day it will be full of secondary fermentation and ruined. For their finale they all fly over me, laughing, splat, splat, splat, yuk!

I know they are beautiful birds!

I know they are one of nature's most spectacular displays!

I know they are supposed to be an endangered species and on the red list!

BUT, I hate every last one of the filthy little blighters.

61 Fertility

As we get towards autumn, my thoughts turn towards fertility. Not my own, you understand, but my cows'. We need to get them back in calf. There are two ways of doing this: naturally and artificially. Both ways have advantages and disadvantages.

The natural way is to put a bull in with them. The advantage with this is that he is watching them all the time and can serve them when they are most fertile. One disadvantage is that Holstein bulls can be a little unpredictable in their temperament and it has never been one of my ambitions to be used as a prayer mat by a 750-kilo bull. The other disadvantage is that because they are unproven, you do not know what traits they will pass on to their daughters. It is a bit like a lucky dip. They could be fine or they could have a temper like Naomi Campbell on a bad day. They could be really showy-type heifers or they could look more like camels.

One of my varied skills as a dairy farmer is that of artificial insemination – pretty impressive, eh?

One of the difficulties of serving the cows artificially is knowing when they are on heat. They only come on heat every twenty-one days, so if you miss a heat, you can lose a lot of time. Some cows are easy to spot and they will happily ride each other all day, come into the yard sweating and bawling with streaks of mud down their flanks and the hair rubbed off their backs. Some cows are very difficult to spot. You will get an inkling that they are on heat and you watch closely for signs, then they turn towards you and give you an Anne Robinson wink. That's good enough for me.

A few years ago we had a cow on heat in the yard. She had a funny look in her eye. It was only when I turned my back that I realised what that look was – lust! I turned around to find her ready to ride me! A lucky escape, I think you will agree. (Mind you, she did have lovely eyes.)

When you have picked out the cow on heat, the next step is to serve her. We have a large flask in the dairy full of liquid nitrogen. This keeps the straws of bull semen at a temperature of about minus 200 degrees Celsius. This is quite cold. The flask contains six canisters. I try not to have more than six bulls stored at any time, or else it gets complicated. There are around a dozen firms trying to sell me bull semen, with several hundred bulls between them. I could probably get a straw of a run-of-the-mill bull or a young untested bull for about £5. However, for a straw of the latest hotshot, such as Picston Shottle or Braedale Goldwyn, I would be looking at £50–60 a straw.

I usually have two or three bulls in the flask for cows, and one for heifers (an easy-calving bull, so the heifers calve easily). Also some straws from a beef bull, for cows we do not wish to breed replacements from.

To make matters more complicated, we can now buy straws of sexed semen, treated so that around ninety per cent of the calves will be female. The drawback of this is that these straws are more expensive and less fertile than normal straws.

I will not go into the details of serving the cows, but while serving them, I like to whisper sweet nothings to them: "There you are, dear, hang on to that."

My usual policy is to start serving just after my birthday, which is on 19 November (cards and presents welcome), and to finish on Valentine's day, when I put a beef bull in with the cows, to catch any I have missed. (I am an old romantic.) These days are not chosen at random, but will ensure the dairy calves are born between the beginning of September and Christmas, so hopefully we can rear them as one batch and get them all to calve in two years' time.

Over the last twelve months our cows' fertility has suffered, and this has long-term repercussions. If the cows do not get in calf when they are supposed to, then in nine months' time, we do not have as many replacement heifers, and the ones we do have are born later, so in turn they don't calve as early as they should. Also, if the cows do not calve, then they will not milk as much, as their peak milk yield is about six weeks after calving. Statistics show that for every day over 365 days between calvings there is a substantial daily financial penalty. This can add up to a lot of money when multiplied by 120 cows.

I have three options that I am considering, to deal with the problem.

1. Carry on as before and hope things improve.
2. Buy a system called Heatime. This would include collars for the cows' necks that would measure their activity. Cows on heat move around a lot more than usual, and this is picked up by the collars. This information would be passed through

a reader onto a monitor, hopefully to tell us when the cows were on heat. I have spoken to several farmers who have installed this system and they all seem very pleased with it.

3. Go on to RMS (reproductive monitoring system). We would have a specialist come in every day to pick out the cows on heat and to serve them. He would put chalk on their backs to see when they were ridden and keep records of cows served and of cows not cycling regularly. With this system, the RMS specialist would ideally look after several herds of cows in close proximity. There are several farms around using this system already.

I doubt that there would be much difference in the cost of options 2 and 3. They will obviously cost me quite a lot, but hopefully not as much in the long term, as option 1.

After writing the above article and after much thought, we purchased the Heatime system. It worked well and we are still using it on the heifers today, some eight years later.

62 Cloning

As the subject of cloning has recently raised its ugly head, with China allegedly looking to clone 100,000 dairy heifers a year to satisfy their desires for dairy products, I thought I would give you my views on the subject. In our herd, in the last thirty years we tried to breed taller cows with tight udders that were up out of the way when they walked through muddy gateways. We also tried to select bulls that would improve yields and to breed for good legs and feet. No matter how good a cow looked, if her feet were no good, then she was no good.

By and large we were successful, with our cows averaging 8000 litres, as opposed to 5000 litres thirty years before. This was not totally due to breeding, but partly due to feeding as well. Our cows were also about a foot taller than their ancestors of thirty years ago. The point I am making is that genetic progress is a long-term project and some cattle breeders have no patience.

Let's suppose I want to breed cows that are very efficient grazers. I would be looking to breed them with wide mouths, as a cow with a four-inch mouth can eat twenty-five per cent more grass than a cow with a three-inch mouth. This would take several generations, i.e. twenty years. Instead of that, imagine if I could clone them with the DNA of a hippopotamus, I could get a cow with a foot-wide mouth in one generation. Of course they could have a predisposition to wallow in mud or any other similar substance that was around. This would mean they would have a lot of fun at Withan Farm during the winter.

I feel that any farmer in this country who is considering cloned animals on his farm is one of three things. Very arrogant, very naïve or very stupid. It is obvious that at the moment the milk-buying public are not willing to accept food from genetically modified sources. He is therefore treating his fellow milk producers with contempt. He is treating the entire dairy industry with contempt and he is treating the general public with contempt.

I would guess that in the next twenty years a certain amount of cloning will take place in a small percentage of top genetic herds, if it becomes politically acceptable to do so. Science is always moving on, and during the 1930s and '40s when artificial insemination was becoming widespread, it must have been completely incomprehensible to a lot of farmers at the time. Similarly, during the 1980s, when sexed semen was being experimented with, I remember thinking, "I cannot see how that is going to work, it will never happen." Yet twenty years later, I was probably using at least twenty-five per cent sexed semen.

63 BRRRRRR

I reach out from the bed, scat over the lamp, knock over a book and at last stop that infernal din. My heart is racing and all my nerves are jangling. I look at the clock. Three o'clock, three o'clock, what does that mean? Oh yes, I have got to look at a cow. My aim now is not to totally wake up if I can avoid it. So I get dressed and walk outside with eyes half closed and mouth open, in zombie mode.

When I get to the cow, she is already calving. I get the calving aid and with a bit of a struggle take the calf. By now, I am wide awake, and on the way back indoors, I have a look at the stars. The North Star is right where it should be and the Plough is tilted at an angle (it does that in the middle of the night, you know).

I get back into bed at three-thirty. Two and a half hours' more sleep – lovely. My body is knackered, but my mind is wide awake and it decides to play "I wonder?"

I wonder why do I like that song by the Manic Street Preachers but I can never remember how it goes? Bom bom de bom. No, that's not it.

I wonder why is it that BP can pollute the Gulf for three months, but I am not allowed to burn a bit of plastic?

I wonder if I give sixty pints of blood and give a load of firewood to the Young Farmers for charity, does that make me a good Samaritan? Or should I send some money to Shelterbox as well?

BRRRRRRRRRRRRRRRRRRRRR.

Six o'clock, time to get up. I bring the cows in and turn the radio on. It's the Manic Street Preachers singing "It's not war, just the end of love". *That's* how it goes. I turn the radio up loud, and as I put the units on, I join in with the chorus: "IT'S NOT WAR, JUST THE END OF LOVE." Another day, another dollar.

64 Peakes

In this book you will come across several references to Peakes. Peakes are a firm who specialise in removing fallen stock, or in other words they pick up dead cows and shoot cows that are ill and unlikely to get better. Doesn't "removing fallen stock" sound better? Most farmers will see a Peakes lorry and automatically think, "I wonder where he is going." I would not put it past some of them to follow it and see!

Peakes will also be used by rumour mongers, as in, "They say Peakes are in there every day," about a farmer who is having a bad streak of luck. Or, as in, "I heard that Peakes had half of them," about a farmer who is selling his cows.

Peakes

Peakes charge £80 to pick up a dead animal and there is no discount if they pick up more than one … Or so I have heard.

They provide an invaluable service, but you do not really want to be seeing them so often that you are on first-name terms with the driver.

65 TB Test

The following article has been bowdlerised by the author (nice word, Brin).

I hardly slept at all that night, tossing and turning, what if … what if … what if we go down, what if we have five reactors, what if we have twenty reactors? It could happen. I saw two badgers in the garden eating apples a month ago. We went down three years ago with two reactors, surely it's not going to happen again? I felt the beads of sweat forming on my forehead and was thankful when the alarm clock sounded. Eating my breakfast was difficult, trying to resist the need to retch with every bite. Stress, stress … those stock market boys ought to do a TB test, then they would know what stress was. All they have to worry about is what they are going to spend their bonus on!

After breakfast, I went outside to bring the heifers in. Has that heifer got a lump on her neck? It looks like it. Oh, sugar, and she's in calf to sexed semen – that will be two replacements gone. Calm down, Brin.

By nine o'clock all the heifers were in and ready to be tested. Where's the vet? He's supposed to be here by nine. Come on, come on. At last, here he is.

As the first heifer headed for the cattle crush, she turned around and jumped a gate, front feet one side, back feet the other. "You ungrateful sods, I do my best for you, I feed you and make sure you have nice grass, I itch your ears and have the vet if you are poorly and this is the way you repay me. Scatting up one of my gates that will cost me eighty quid to replace. You make me sick!"

TB Test

We sent her around again, and three at a time they got corralled behind the gate and then into the crush. Everything went fairly smoothly for some time, then the vet shouted, "Stop that one!"

"Oh no, I bet she's got it. Sugar!"

"Alright, you can let her go."

Thank goodness for that.

We brought the next three in and then SMACK, aaaargh! "You bitch, right below the knee, number 2563. I will remember you, you, you, you … bitch."

"Are you alright?"

"Of course I am not alright. Do I look alright?!"

After a couple of minutes I managed to stand up and tried to ignore the relieved smirks.

"Lucky it wasn't any higher, or you'd be singing soprano."

"Yes, yes, very funny."

We finished with the small calves, and apart from raking my shins with their sharp hooves, they went through very well. The last calf went through, and then …

"All clear, no lumps at all."

We all washed up and then went inside for a cup of coffee and a bit of heavy cake, with me hobbling along painfully and slowly at the rear.

It had been a very, very good day!

66 Stupidity

Once upon a time, there was a cow who died of stupidity.

She slipped over in the yard and could not get up. Not a bad case of the splits, but enough to put me on edge. We managed to roll her into the loader bucket and carried her down to the Parc Bullock, a six-acre, fairly level field. She immediately got to her feet, and I thought, "Ideal. I will leave her there for a couple of days until she is steady on her feet and then bring her back into the yard."

But, oh no, Sod's law kicked in and she decided to commit "Harry Carry" in a four-feet-deep ditch. We managed to get her out, but it was obvious that she had "reached the end of her useful life", so I "hastened her passage to a better world" (that's a euphemism for shooting her). While cows are lying around the place, dead or dying, they remind you of your failings every time you see them, but once Peakes have removed them, you can forget about them until you get the Peakes bill at the end of the month.

We have had some stupid cows, but this one took stupidity to a whole new level.

67 Costs

When I am rambling on in these articles, I suppose I should make it clear that I am writing about my own experiences and thoughts and these are not necessarily the same as any other dairy farmer who happens to reside in Meneage.

This month I thought I would write about costs of production, i.e. for every litre that we send off the farm, what the costs for that litre are. I have looked back at my records since my brother and myself split our partnership around 1996. At that time, our average milk price for the year was about 26 p/litre. Today, fifteen years later, that bright-eyed young man who used to look out of the mirror at me in the mornings, has turned into a bleary-eyed, wrinkly-faced old hasbeen. In the meantime our milk price for the last year has been around 22 p/litre.

To be vulgar for a minute and to try and explain the difference, let's assume that for all of those fifteen years, we have sent off 800,000 litres of milk (this being our current level of production). In 1996, this would amount to milk sales of £208,000. Yet today, fifteen years later, this amount of milk brings in £176,000. So today, fifteen years later, we would be £32,000/year worse off, assuming our production had stayed the same.

I know these are large figures, but I think they are easier to put into context than pence/litre, and please remember, that TURNOVER IS VANITY BUT PROFIT IS SANITY.

Now, to return to costs, I do not suppose that any of you are paying less for your electricity than you did fifteen years ago, or petrol, or heating, or rates, or maintenance of your houses, or practically anything. It is the same in farming, with costs going up year on year.

Costs

Contrary to popular belief, grass does not "just grow" but needs to be fertilised, the weeds sprayed and every few years the fields need reseeding, plus the costs of growing maize. These costs add up to about 2.4 p/litre. If we take this off our milk price of 22 p/litre, we are left with 19.6p. Next we come to feed costs: this is the concentrate that we feed to our cows, to balance the forage. This equates to approximately 6.5 p/litre, leaving us with 13.1p. We then add in our vet costs. Those of you who have pets will know that these can be considerable. For us, these can add up to £2000 in a bad month. This is not just emergencies, but routine visits, to keep on top of any problems, pregnancy test cows, vaccines for leptospirosis, BVD and blue tongue, etc. 1.1 p/litre, leaving us with 12.1p. Semen costs 0.4p, bedding costs 0.4p, electricity 0.7p, professional fees (accountant, etc.) 0.4p, insurance 0.4p. When we take these off, we are left with 9.8p. We now put in labour costs of 2.5p, for our workman and my son. We are left with 6.3p. We now take off my living expenses of approx 2p (I really must stop taking these expensive foreign holidays and stop the fast living, the drinking and the gambling). Anyway, that leaves us with 4.2p. Next we add in rent of 1p, leaving us with 3.2p. Isn't it amazing how quickly the pennies disappear!

Our next costs are machinery and contracting. Unfortunately, due to the layout of our land, half of it is two miles away on the other side of Manaccan, and these costs are exceptionally high. When we pull slurry to my brother's land, we load up the tanker and head up to the top of the lane with the tractor groaning with the strain. We reach the top and turn left down Carnbarges Hill, brakes squealing in protest all the way down, change down several gears at the bottom and grind our way to the top, change up at Landrivick and try to get up enough momentum in that short downhill run to enable us to get up the short hill just before Tregithew. We then go around the next lot of corners, concentrating hard so as not to mount a sports car that might be coming in the other direction. Straight across the crossroads, past Tregonwell, waving to Dennis and Daphne as we go by. We then come to a straight, level bit of road, where with a bit of luck we might get the tractor to top speed. Then it is down through Manaccan, past the New Inn, brakes squealing once more, over the bridge, turn right by my brother's vegetable stall, grind our way up the hill, spread the slurry and then home again ready to start the next load. As you can imagine, this puts considerable strain on the brakes, the gears, the clutch, the tyres and the driver. A point to note is that my neighbour, whose land is all in one place, can spread as much slurry in a day as we can in a week. In the summer, when we are doing silage, it is the same situation. We have seven tractors and trailers pulling, each one costing us £25/hour, making a total of £175/hour, and when you multiply this for a twelve-hour day, we will call it £2000/day for easy reckoning. If we multiply this by three cuts of grass silage plus two days of pulling maize, we end up talking of around £10,000 or 1.2p/litre just for carrying the stuff, before we begin to add in the costs of the forage harvester.

I hope you can begin to see that in the long term this is unsustainable. So what are our options? 1) We increase our herd significantly to spread our costs over more litres, 2) we cut our costs significantly to increase our profitability, 3) we get a large price increase, and 4) we give up milking cows.

For either of the first two options to work we need to get hold of another hundred acres that is touching Withan, and quite frankly that is not going to happen. We have the river hemming us in on one side and three fellow dairy farmers hemming us in on the other sides. We therefore come to option 3. When I talk about a large price increase, I am not talking about 1 or 2 p/litre, but 8 to 10 p/litre to bring the price up to at least 30p. I am afraid that this will not happen, because while there are mugs like me willing to work for next to nothing because "it is a way of life", then the large retailers are quite willing to let us. I know that I have done all I can to raise the milk price. I have stood in the middle of Truro, handing out cheese to the general public, telling them the milk price needs to go up. I have met a solicitor working for the NFU and showed him all my figures for twenty years and explained that the milk price needs to go up. I have demonstrated outside various milk factories in the past, holding banners saying the milk price needs to go up. I go to the Milk Link meeting at Scorrier every six months, stand up and say the milk price needs to go up. I went to the Milk Link AGM a couple of years ago and stood up and said the milk price needs to go up. The response I get at these meetings, from the chairman down, is, "We are building a strong business, blah, blah, blah, price of turnips, blah, blah, blah, working twenty-four hours a day, blah, blah, blah, to create a sustainable milk price, blah, blah, blah, jam tomorrow, blah, blah, blah, jam tomorrow, blah, blah, blah!"

We then come to option 4. We give up milking cows. Last week we decided that this was the right option for us. A decision I thought I would never take. I went for a long walk and when I came back, Ruth asked me if I had found any answers. I replied that I did not think there were any. I then sat down and for two hours I cried like a baby. (I know – how pathetic is that?)

It is now four-fifty in the morning, on 24 September 2010, and we will be reading our TB test later on this morning. If we go clear, the cows will be advertised in the *West Briton* next week and by the end of next month they will be "up the road". And I will be another ex dairy farmer.

I realise that there are people out there who know the answer to all my problems, but I have not had the benefit of their wisdom yet, and if I am really lucky, that's the way it will stay.

A final thought: when you watch Tesco's adverts (every little helps) and Asda price, bom bom, remember that there is no such thing as cheap food, and out there *someone* is paying!

We had a clear TB test and I arranged for all my cows, heifers and calves to be sold at Truro Market on 19 October.

The milk price on average is now less than when we decided enough was enough and to call it a day. I do not know how many dairy farmers can cope with such prices.

68 Cow Sale

For all you adrenalin junkies out there, I have found a new form of extreme sport. You can forget bungee jumping or white-water rafting: trimming cows for a sale is the in thing, and you are almost guaranteed to get hurt.

Back to the beginning, after we had the clear TB test and had contacted the auctioneers to arrange the sale of the cows, we decided to have the cows clipped to make them look their best for the sale. This is like giving them a number 1 crew cut all over their heads, their top line and their nether regions. There were two men called Fred doing the clipping, plus two more helpers. Fred 1 was clipping the udders and belly of the cows and Fred 2 was clipping the heads. Fred 2 was the first one to come to grief. He was clipping a cow's neck when she brought her head up and crushed his arm between her head and an iron bar on the cattle crush. He removed his arm, wincing in considerable pain, and called the cow a name (and it wasn't Daisy). I am afraid I blushed – I had never heard such language!

Meanwhile Fred 1 was taking his life is his own hands, trimming away at the udders. Well, I wouldn't have liked it. One of our cows took exception to such treatment and kicked him in the chest and for ten minutes he was unable to call her anything at all.

They were clipping on the Friday for thirteen hours and on the Saturday for over sixteen hours. Two long days for all of us.

Among the other things we had to do were to pregnancy test all the cows and heifers that were supposed to be in calf (there were two that were not in calf that I was not aware of). We then had to check the freshly calved cows to make sure they were clean (i.e. ready to be served). We then had to get all of our data from National Milk Records. We had been milk recording for at least thirty years, so there was a lot of data. This told us not only how much milk our cows have given and what quality, for all of their lactations, but also all of their dams' lactations and their grand dams' lactations. I have to say, it looked pretty impressive. The next thing was to check the ear tags. All animals must have an ear tag in each ear when they go to market (if not, we will be hung, drawn and quartered). We probably had to send away for at least thirty replacement tags. Finally, the auctioneers, Lodge and Thomas, sent us the draft sale catalogue and I had to check through it for mistakes and omissions. I found three pages' worth and these were put right before the finished catalogue came out.

On Monday 18 October, three lorries turned up and carried the dry cows and the heifers up to Truro market. Seven loads went up on the Monday. On Monday night, we carried some hay up to the market to feed the animals that were there. Fred and Fred were up there, washing and shampooing them, making them look as good as possible. That night the milking cows were milked at midnight, thus ensuring that when the sale started at midday their udders were full of milk and they would look as good as they possibly could. The lorries turned up again on Tuesday morning at five a.m. and then returned for the final two loads at seven a.m.

I arrived at the market at about ten o'clock. Fred and Fred were back again, washing and shampooing once more. I had a final check of the catalogue to point out any problem cows, e.g. three-quarter cows (cows that only have milk in three quarters) or cows that would not lie in cubicles. We then went out the back to look at "our herd" for the last time. They looked immaculate and we were very proud of what we had achieved.

Cow Sale

I stood in the ring, with our son David sending them around. The first cow in the ring was a second calver giving nine gallons of milk a day and looking a picture. She sold for 1200 guineas and set the tone for the rest of the sale, with the majority of the animals selling really well and buyers from as far away as Totnes and Boscastle and as near as St Martin and Manaccan.

The sale finished at around three-thirty with the baby calves selling last and again selling really well. We were very well supported by our friends and neighbours and we really appreciate that. All that was left was to think, thirty-five years of dairy farming gone in three and a half hours! We returned home about six o'clock, mentally and physically shattered. As I came in the door I glanced at the noticeboard, and there was my son's "to do" list:

1. Sort cows' feed barrier by shed
2. Mend wood on dry cow barrier
3. Concrete cow shed wall
4. Build up wall in top cow shed
5. Tipping troughs (get)
6. ...

69 Protesting

During 1996, we were receiving 26 p/litre for our milk. Ten years later we were receiving less than two thirds of that price. Some of the advice I was given was that you should concentrate on what you could change and not worry about what you could not. That was not my attitude. My attitude was that someone was creaming up to ten pence a litre off my milk cheque and I should do all I could to stop them. If I was not going to stand up for my business, then who was?

Consequently, I protested, with many others. We protested at Truro, where we handed out cheese to the public and explained our grievances. We protested at the Labour Party Conference, held in Bournemouth, walking through the streets carrying banners. We also protested at various milk factories: the Dairy Crest factory at Davidstow and the milk factory at Totnes. These were evening visits and were nearly two hours from Withan, which meant late nights, not really compatible with early mornings.

I remember at Totnes we were addressed by the chief executive of the company. I realised that evening that there were no ethics or moral standards in most big business. I despised what that man said and I despised what he stood for.

Did I enjoy protesting?

No, I did not. I would rather have been home cleaning out drains.

Did my protests do any good?

My ultimate protest was to stop milking: that obviously stopped anyone from creaming off my milk cheque. For the industry as a whole, in 1996 the milk price was 26 p/litre, more than the average dairy farmer is receiving today!

I do not know what the answers are, but I think I am well out of it.

10 After the Sale

After the sale, back at Cold Comfort Farm, once the cows had gone and the dust settled, we decided to go in for contract heifer rearing. I have got no interest in beef cattle or crop farming. Beside which, Withan is not suitable for anything but stock farming, because of the hills. We currently have around 123 heifers here, all from one farm. They come at about twelve months old and I look after them, inject them if they need injecting, inseminate them when they are on heat and send them back home a fortnight before they are due to calve. The advantage for the owner of the heifers is that it frees up land, in order to up the numbers of his dairy cows, and eases the management, as he does not have to think about the heifers. The disadvantage for him is that he has to pay me.

We are also picking up a bit of work locally, pulling silage, tractor work or helping with stock. I could probably be milking fourteen times a week for other farmers if I wanted, but so far I have resisted the temptation.

I think the worst time for me was last month when the milking parlour was sold and went to Wellington in Somerset. When I go into that shed now, there is just a large hole in the floor and it is like stepping onto something that is not there. It gets me every time. Looking back, I know it was the right decision for us, but that does not make it any easier.

71 TB — Looking Back

Tuberculosis and badgers is still an emotive subject, with practically everyone having an opinion and practically everyone being an expert on the subject.

Whenever we had a positive TB result, we would have a D.E.F.R.A. vet come out with several forms to fill out. There was one question: "Are you taking precautions to keep badgers off your property?" They might just as well have asked us if we were taking precautions to stop the tide coming in! With at least a mile boundary, we would need a fence similar to that surrounding Culdrose Air Station, and unfortunately we do not have the same budget as Culdrose. We would always have a different vet for every case we had and I would always take the opportunity to ask them, "Where is it coming from?" The answer was always, unequivocally, "Badgers." Although they were quite happy to tell me that, I never got the impression they would stand and say the same thing into a microphone. Part of their terms of employment, I always assumed.

Some time after our first reactor, I thought I ought to learn more about the disease and so I went to an NFU meeting on TB, held at Truro. There was one man there who seemed to be talking a lot of common sense. I saw him after the meeting and he agreed to come down to Withan and have a look around the area.

Several weeks later, we spent a day looking around Withan and the surrounding area, examining badger setts, some that I knew were there and some that I did not. My visitor's theory was that you could tell where the sick badgers were, because they would not clean the entrance to their setts and would let weeds grow. They would not move far from their setts and would defecate almost right outside them.

His theory sounded perfectly logical to me, and I have been thinking even more about it in the last three weeks, because I have had toothache (sympathy welcome). In the past three weeks I have not run downstairs, thrown open the door and in a pleasing baritone sung, "There's a bright golden haze in the meadow," picked up a broom and swept the yard. In the last three weeks, I have fallen out of bed, slouched outside, done what had to be done, come in, downed a couple of Nurofen, sat in the armchair and wallowed in my own misery.

His other theory, after looking at all the setts, was that the healthy badgers were driving the sick badgers out of the area, towards the river, where they dug small setts because there was nowhere else for them to go. Again this seemed perfectly logical as, at the time, four farms in our village that bordered the river went down with TB within a month of each other.

On a neighbouring farm they have lost another eight animals to TB this year, but thankfully have had a clear test last week. Another friend has lost seventeen animals since the beginning of the year and is waiting their next test with trepidation.

Thankfully, at the moment we are free of TB, but for how long? There are at least seventy badger holes on Withan alone, in around half a dozen setts, and that, to my unscientific, but logical mind is far, far too many.

72 Heifer Treatments

November at Withan, we have 145 heifers inside for the winter, with just fifteen in-calf heifers left outside on grass. In the past seventeen days, I have served thirty-seven heifers with sexed semen and hopefully most of them will hold to that first service. Since bringing them in, we have treated them with a wormer, which is a pour-on treatment, which makes it easy to administer. We have also given them a flukicide. This is a drench, which is not so easy to administer. These treatments will stop any worms or liver fluke upsetting the animals and stopping them from growing properly.

We have also vaccinated all the breeding-age heifers against BVD and leptospirosis. If asked which vaccine is most important, I would always say leptospirosis, because this is a zoonotic disease and can be passed on to humans. It is passed to humans very distastefully by a drop of infected urine getting in your eye. This might sound extremely unlikely, but when milking in a parlour with twenty-four cows standing three feet above you, a urine shower is an occupational hazard.

I know several farmers and vets who have caught leptospirosis and the symptoms are the same as a severe form of flu, with severe headaches and liver problems. Thankfully all the people I know who have caught it, have made a full recovery.

73 In the Bleak Mid Winter

In the bleak mid winter
Brindley started to moan,
His chilblains are giving him jip
And he's chilled to the bone.

In the bleak mid winter,
Brindley slipped on the ice,
He smashed the ice with the back of his head
And that wasn't very nice.

In the bleak mid winter,
Milk tanker could not get around,
Brindley was totally cheesed off
As six thousand litres spilled out on the ground.

In the bleak mid winter,
A cow started to groan,

Brindley tried to help her
But no good, she's dead as a stone.

In the bleak mid winter,
Brindley's hoping for sun.
He thinks that ice and cold and snow
Are not a lot of fun.

74 London Trip

A fortnight before Christmas, Ruth and I decided to have a day or two away from the farm and travel to London.

Our holiday started in Redruth train station, where there is a large photograph showing the weekly exodus of hundreds of Cornishmen to the mines of South Africa in the early 1900s. Their wives and families are looking down from a nearby bank. This photo always has a poignant effect on me, as my great-grandfather, Athanasius Jenkin, travelled to South Africa to the mines and it is quite probable that his journey started at Redruth station.

During the five-hour train journey to London, I spent my time looking out of the windows at the farms we were passing. The thousands of acres on the Somerset Levels that are still under water after all the recent rain, wondering if the land underneath the water will produce anything in the next year, or will the grass be drowned or poisoned by all the pollution in the flood water? The fields of maize around Taunton that have not been harvested yet, wondering if they will ever be harvested, and if not, what the farmer would be feeding his stock that winter. The muddy tracks the tractor had made driving into the fields to feed outwintered stock. The small drokes made in the hilly fields, where the rain had eroded the soil away. The fields of winter corn peeping through the ground in their rows, with the tramlines clearly visible, giving the farmer clear guidance where to drive in the spring.

As we pulled into Paddington, past the many miles of graffiti and the highrise flats with football banners hanging from them, I found myself wondering, what did "normal" passengers see when looking out of the train window?

75 Heifers Dying

Since we sold our cows and have had just dairy heifers on the farm, we have been quite lucky in the fact that none of them has managed to find a reason to pass away. Apart from three that were culled because of TB, and I do not count these, as at the moment TB is an occupational hazard. This lack of dying is not from a want of trying on their part, with several of them managing to get into the slurry pit and attempting to drown themselves, but thankfully after a few minutes getting out again. Other heifers have jumped gates or got tangled up in the cubicles, in a vain attempt to break a leg or hurt themselves in a life-threatening way.

I was feeling quite smug about this lack of casualties, until one day last autumn when we lost two in one day. The first heifer had slipped over in the cubicle shed the previous day and done the splits. We followed our usual protocol for this type of incident: pick her up in the loader bucket and put her in a loose house on straw, give her some silage and water. Usually they are up and about after a couple of days. I went to see her the next morning and she was stone dead. Feeling very bad, I phoned Peakes to come and pick her up. I then went to see the heifers in the field. One was lying down looking very sorry for herself – she had not been thriving like the rest and had lost condition but I did not think she was that bad. I called the vet, but he could not do anything for her except put her down. By this time Peakes had been, so feeling even worse, I called them and asked them to come again.

This is the time that the old platitudes come to mind.

Where you have got livestock, you will get deadstock!

Heifers Dying

Only them that has them, can lose them!

Looking back, I feel there was nothing I could have done in either case and it was just coincidence that both died on the same day.

16 Christmas Switch

I thought I would tell you what happens on a dairy farm at Christmas. Luckily, cows have a switch in their left ear that you would not even notice if you didn't know it was there. This switch has two settings. Active and hibernate. When you switch to hibernate, the cow will lie in the cubicle, go to sleep and not need to eat, muck or be milked again until you turn the switch back to active again. Our usual routine is to start them hibernating on 23 December and turn them back to active on 3 January. This ensures that we get a fortnight's holiday at Christmas, the same as a large section of the population.

Oh dear, I seem to have been visiting Cloud Cuckoo Land again! I will start again.

Christmas Switch

As it is now coming up to Christmas, I thought I would tell you what happens on a dairy farm at Christmas. What we try to do is to accomplish as much as possible on Christmas Eve. This means ensuring the heifers and dry cows have enough straw and silage for two or three days. We still check them, but it probably saves half an hour's work.

We know, as all dairy farmers know, that if something is going to go wrong, it will go wrong on Christmas Day. In the past this has taken the form of coming out on Christmas morning and finding two tractors with punctures. Another time, coming home in the evening to milk and finding rainwater running through a hole in the roof, straight into our electric box – not an ideal situation. In the week before Christmas, therefore, we try to anticipate what may go wrong and fix it, instead of thinking that it will probably be alright till the New Year.

On this farm, Christmas would start at about five-forty a.m., when the children came into our room to show us what Father Christmas has brought them. When I say "children", they are now eighteen, seventeen and fourteen, but tradition is tradition. I would then go out about six o'clock and start the milking. David, my son, would go out the same time and scrape out the cubicles, mix up feed for the cows, feed the calves, etc., and with a bit of luck, we would be finished just after nine o'clock.

The next few hours are spent in a traditional way, visiting relatives, eating turkey with all the trimmings and opening presents. I think last year we were twenty-five for Christmas dinner (Ruth and I have both got large families).

At about five o'clock, we would head home to do the afternoon work, the cows would be milked again, the calves fed, the rest of the stock checked, and hopefully by about seven we'd be finished. This was quite good in some ways, as by the time we got indoors, we were wide awake and ready to start on cold turkey and mince pies.

Something to remember is that on the Lizard peninsula there are still over thirty dairy herds, all being milked twice on Christmas day. There are milk tanker drivers picking up the milk and there are vets on call in case of emergencies. One of my neighbours had the vet out on Christmas Day to do an emergency caesarean on a cow. As I said before, if anything can go wrong, it will on Christmas Day.

If you are reading this near Christmas, I would like to wish you and yours a happy and peaceful Christmas.

77 Slurry

This winter, due to it being so wet, we had only managed to spread ten loads of slurry by the middle of February. If we go out into the fields with the slurry tanker when it is too wet, we can make a real mess of the fields and leave ruts that are almost impossible to remove without reseeding the field. Our slurry pit was full to bursting, so we took the decision to have a contractor in to empty the pit. They came with an umbilical system. They had one tractor parked next to the slurry pit, pumping the slurry through a flexible pipe to another tractor in the field, which was spreading the slurry. They managed to spread about sixty-five acres in three days, putting on over 4000 gallons an acre and totalling nearly 300,000 gallons spread. All this without ripping up the fields. It would have taken me nearly three weeks to spread that amount of slurry – if the weather was favourable. We had the slurry analysed. There was 2 units of nitrogen per 1000 gallons, 2.5 units of phosphate and 13 units of potash. We can then take this into consideration when applying artificial fertiliser and hopefully save a bit of money.

I did not think there was any downside to this way of spreading slurry – that is, until the bill came!

78 Bude

A few weeks ago Ruth and I had the chance of a few days away. It was a choice between Bermuda, Bahamas, Bali and Bude. We went to Bude. By an extraordinary coincidence, the Cornish Grassland Society had organised two farm walks on one of the days we were away, not far from where we were staying. On the Tuesday, I set off for the farm walk at Crackington Haven. Ruth, strangely enough, thought she would rather go shopping in Bude for the day. At the farm walk there were around two hundred farmers from all over Cornwall and Devon. It is a strange thing, but most farmers (myself included) when given the chance of a day off like nothing better than to spend the day looking around someone else's farm.

The first farm walk was a three-hundred-cow dairy farm above Crackington Haven. Rex Ward, the farmer, took us up to the highest coastal cliffs in Cornwall and told us from there we could see as far as Hartland Point to the north and Tintagel to the south. Unfortunately, we could only see a hundred yards in any direction, due to the fog.

The second farm walk was a thousand-acre beef and sheep farm on the Cornwall–Devon border, owned by John Medland. Both farm walks were very interesting and enjoyable.

For the other four days that we were away, we walked the coast path, managing to get from Bude to Port Isaac and seeing some spectacular scenery in the process. We have almost finished walking the north Cornish coast now and hope to complete it this summer.

79 Splits

Sometimes a cow will fall over in the yard. This can be for a variety of reasons. She may be on heat and have been ridden by another cow, she might have just calved and be a bit unsteady, she may have had a fight with another cow, or the yard may be very slippery because of the weather conditions. If we are lucky, she will get up straight away. If she looks a bit unsteady, I will scuttle around the yard, with my arms underneath her, looking like I have an udder fetish (as if!). I am hoping that if she slips again, my svelte ninety-five kilos will be able to stop her six hundred kilos from falling again.

If we are unlucky, she will do the splits. This is where her legs will either slip out behind her, or out sideways. She will be lying in manure (we have a more colloquial name for it, but for the purposes of decorum, we will call it manure), and instead of lying still, she will usually struggle and make matters worse and get herself covered all over with manure. Probably eighty per cent of cows that have done the splits badly will not get over it, but we persist in "giving them a chance". This entails rolling a six-hundred-kilo cow, covered in manure, into the loader bucket (ensuring that we too are covered in manure) and transporting her into the field behind the house. A field also known as Death Row! We then pay the vet something extortionate to come and inject her with an anti-inflammatory drug and some other concoction and hope for the best. We spend the next week carrying water and food to her and turning her over to prevent sores. During this time she will gradually work her way to the bottom of the field. If she has not stood up by the time she reaches the bottom of the field, we have to admit defeat and call "The Grim Reaper", i.e. Peakes.

To my mind, the splits are the worst thing that can happen to a cow. The odd few will get over it and rejoin the herd, but for most it will be terminal. It is extremely stressful for me as well, and I am left tearing my hair out and wondering how I can stop it happening again.

80 Four Years On

I feel that I was probably genetically predisposed to be a dairy farmer, as my father was a dairy farmer, both my grandfathers were dairy farmers, all four of my uncles were dairy farmers and so on, back into the previous generations. At the time of selling the cows, the feeling in my head was of not quite measuring up, or of being slightly inadequate. These feelings caused a certain amount of depression in me for some time.

Looking back, some four years later, with, I hope, a clearer and more rational head, I realise that I was a damn good dairy farmer and that circumstances and a particularly difficult-to-manage farm were to blame for my untimely exit from the dairy industry.

During the past four years, Ruth and I have been walking the South-west Coastal Path when we have time and I realise that this would probably not have happened if I was still milking, as if we had a day off, I would probably have been too knackered to walk from Crackington Haven to Boscastle, or Portscatho to Portloe.

Although happy enough in the past to milk my cows and for some years to do fourteen milkings in a week and for fifty-one weeks in the year, I have never had any desire to milk anyone else's cows. In fact in the past four years I have only milked once and that was only because my cousin needed a hand after a cow had cracked a couple of his ribs!

After selling our cows, our worry was that the dairy industry would turn around and herald a golden decade of sustainable prices and massive profits and we would be left cursing that we left the industry at the wrong time. Obviously, this has not happened and once again the milk price is heading south at an alarming rate with no sign of bottoming out as yet. With, as I understand it, a price crash of around 6.5 p/litre, the average producer, milking 130 cows averaging 8000 litres with an annual output of around one million litres (easy reckoning), makes a drop in income of approximately £65,000 over the year, turning, for many producers, I would imagine, a healthy profit into a substantial loss and necessitating a dry-mouthed phone call to the bank manager to ask for a substantial rise in the overdraft facility and to explain why the carefully worked-out budget for the year looks like a work of complete fiction.

After reading that farm borrowings had reached a new high of £15.9 billion at the end of August 2014 and seeing dairy farmers once more protesting about milk prices, and having made the ultimate dairy protest myself four years ago by selling my cows, I realise that nothing has really changed and the industry still has no financial stability. Surely dairy farming, as any business, should be a means to an end and not an end in itself?

81 Wedding Shopping

What is keeping me up at night at the moment is the rapid approach of my eldest daughter's wedding. The worst of it is that she is moving across the water. Alright, so it is just the Helford river and the fact I can see the farm she is moving to from our top fields makes no difference (in fact if I could yodel, my future son-in-law would probably hear me). My mind is full of marquees, bridesmaids, generators and speeches, mine in particular. Last week, as part of the preparations, I was summoned to go off "mother of the bride" shopping. I missed two Six Nations games in the process, surely dedication beyond the call of duty. We meandered through Cornwall, visiting various expensive dress shops before ending up in Saltash. Here Ruth started trying on several smart suits and hats (John Charles, for those in the know). I sat down and every so often gave my valued(?) opinion. Then it happened. I expect you know. During a lull in the proceedings, the shop assistant turned to me and said, "I take it you are a farmer?"

How the heck do they know?

I had a shower before I left home and I am sure there were no lingering traces of Eau de Bovine or Heifer No. 5 left on me. When I have a beastly job to do, I wear gloves, so the creases in my hands are not cagged with ingrained dirt, so it was not that. Did the slight limp where a heifer recently kicked me in the knee give the game away? Or maybe the grimace I gave when standing up, as my back gave me another twinge, as a reminder of fifty-four years of abuse? Maybe it was my rugged good looks and healthy complexion. Ruth says it was none of the above. She says it was the look on my face when I heard the price of those outfits that she was trying on: "HOW much?"

I think at the moment we are in control, but 15 June seems to be approaching rather rapidly. Hence the waking up at night in a cold sweat, and murmuring bits of a speech that is churning around in my head. All I have left to do is paint the house and the outbuildings, sort out the garden, tidy up the yard, get the grass to grow, cut the silage, pray for fine weather, level the car park gateway and make direction signs.

I feel it is so much less stressful having the reception at home!!!

82 British Grassland Summer Meeting

I thought I would tell you about my "busman's holiday" during July. We were based at the Lanhydrock Hotel and Golf Club for three nights (I know, but sometimes you have to slum it!). The occasion was the British Grassland Society's AGM and summer meeting and was held in North Cornwall in 2015. There were delegates from all over England, Wales, Scotland and Ireland.

We arrived on Sunday afternoon, and after a three-course meal there was a presentation from the four Cornish Grassland Societies – Bude, North Cornwall, East Cornwall and West Cornwall – along with musical interludes by Launceston Male Voice Choir. I gave the presentation on behalf of West Cornwall, which was a talk on the area and the agriculture.

Over the next three days, we visited eight farms, some dairy, some beef, some very intensive, some very extensive, some conventional and some organic, some owned and some rented. All different, but all exceptionally well managed, with a keen focus on grassland management.

On the Tuesday evening, the gala dinner of the British Grassland Society was held at Lanhydrock, and by a quirk of circumstances, I found myself chairing the evening, with 170 present (no pressure then!).

On the Wednesday, the final farm we visited overlooked Polzeath on the North Cornwall coast. The sun came out for the first time that week, and with the sea in the background it showed our visitors Cornwall at its best.

Looking back, it was quite daunting, giving the presentation and chairing the dinner, but I am glad that I was given the opportunity and I am very glad I took it.

83 Geoffrey

At the moment at Withan we have about 150 heifers. We also have a Hereford bull, called Geoffrey. The scores are thirty pregnancies to Geoffrey and a rather magnificent gold-winning sixty-nine pregnancies to me. We serve the heifers between 20 October and 20 April, as this ensures that the calves are born from the end of July till the end of January. Unfortunately, Geoffrey cannot get this fact through his thick head, and rather like the man in the Milk Tray advert, feels he must get through any barrier that stands in his way to deliver the goods.

Geoffrey is smashing up some of our gates. He starts by resting his great fat head on them and then when they buckle, he thinks he can jump them or rather scramble over them. He also likes to deliver more than chocolates when he gets there. It is *very*

annoying. Each gate will probably cost me around £80 to replace and he is mucking up our calving pattern as well.

We try and keep him with the in-calf heifers and well away from the younger heifers but he is quite determined. All part of the many joys of farming, I suppose.

84 Daffodils

During this spring, besides looking after my own farm, I have been doing some work at the daffodil farm at Bosahan. This has meant the alarm clock going off at five o'clock and then scraping up and feeding the heifers and sorting out any problems, and aiming to get to Bosahan around seven-thirty, leaving Ruth to finish off the yard work.

My job at Bosahan was to deliver empty trays to the fields and then collect the daffodils from the fields and carry them back to the farm, with a trailer on the back of our tractor. This trailer holds 280 trays of daffodils, with each tray holding 100 bunches of daffodils – 28,000 bunches each trip. Back at the farm, it was a case of labelling each pallet of flowers with the name of the team that picked them, the variety of daff and the day they were picked, trying hard not to get confused. Talking of varieties, I thought a daffodil was a daffodil, but apparently not.

I picked up Jedna, Tamsyn, Tamara, Rosenwyn, Adventure and Veryan.

I picked up Bonallan, Karenza, California, Dutch Master, Sealing Wax, Granilly and Dellen.

I picked up Planet, Carlton, Mando, Camelot, Standard Value and Golden Ducat.

I picked up Number 9, Number 39 and finally St Patrick's Day.

There are over three hundred acres of daffodils grown by the farm in over fifty fields around the peninsula, from Manaccan to Gunwalloe to Trevenen. This acreage of daffs takes around two hundred pickers (mainly Lithuanians and Romanians) and three tractors carting the flowers back.

As you can imagine, it has been very wet and windy this spring and in some fields there were patches that were very steep and muddy. It was a work of art to avoid these muddy patches, but, by either luck or brilliant tractor-driving skills (I will let you make your own mind up which), I managed to avoid getting stuck and having the embarrassment of being pulled out by another tractor.

It was quite a difficult season, with the early flowers held back and then all heading in February, making it an extremely intensive month.

For myself, it was a hard few weeks, with long hours, but it was quite interesting to get involved in another sphere of agriculture right on my doorstep, which I knew nothing about.

85 Insemination

The other morning, I was serving a heifer, as is my wont. I was giving her a straw of Picasso Red and subconsciously talking to her at the same time: "That's right, my sweetheart, you just keep still for a few more minutes, that's the girl, thaaaaat's the girl."

Ruth was squeegeeing slurry nearby. She looked up and said, "You never speak to me like that!"

Heck, I thought. Careful, Brin, that's a minefield, where do I go with that? "Nobody can wear oilers like you can, my little Sugar Plum"? Or "Morning, my prairie flower, you look lovely when you're holding a squeegee"? Steady, Brin, better say nothing and be thought a fool than to open your mouth and remove all doubt.

Give it time. Give it time.

Luckily, Ruth was only joking … I think!

86 New Bull

Last November, Geoffrey the Hereford bull went up the road, due to his penchant for wrecking gates, climbing through hedges, ravishing underage heifers and siring enormous calves. Today I am pleased to announce there is a new kid in town.

He is a North Devon bull and as yet without a name. When he arrived we were going to put him in the cattle crush and vaccinate him for BVD, but he arrived a bit stressed and was clearly not going to cooperate. We then decided to put him in with the heifers, let him calm down and get over the journey. A week later, I managed to give him his vaccination as he was lying down. Less stress for both of us. Unfortunately, last month a farmer in Wales was killed by a bull during a TB test, which reinforces the lesson that no bull is to be played with or taken for granted.

Cows & Catastrophes

The first day here the bull managed to get his head stuck in the feed barrier due to his massive head and neck and his stubs of horns. Thankfully he soon learned and now he turns his head on one side and gets one horn through and then turns his head the other way to get the other horn through. He seems to be working at the moment and the next step will be pregnancy testing the heifers he has served, and hoping he does not start jumping gates.

87 Dairy Farmers Anonymous

I have a confession to make. My name is Brindley Hosken and I am a dairy farmer. It is an affliction that runs in the family. My father and both my grandfathers both suffered from it. Looking back, it started when I was very young, with a toy farmyard and plastic cows, all very innocent, but it was just stoking the flames. As I got older, it became more of an obsession: mixing with other dairy farmers, spending my waking hours dairy farming and spending all my money on dairy farming. Sheds, milk quota, cows. No vice was out of bounds. What was the fascination? It might have been the thrill of opening the milk cheque on the seventeenth of every month, or the satisfaction of being on top of the job, or watching the cows cudding in a fresh field of grass, or seeing calves born and knowing that they would one day join the herd. It might have been spending time outside with the sun on my back, or the beauty of the countryside around me. Phew, I can feel myself start to sweat.

I decided I had to stop before the obsession made me ill. I came off cold turkey, deciding to sell the herd and doing it in less than a month. It was four years before the pangs stopped, and I am always aware of temptation.

If any of you reading this notice the same symptoms in yourself and are wondering if you have a problem, the things to look out for are:

At a party, do you automatically gravitate towards other dairy farmers in the room and spend the night discussing the milk price and bactoscans?

If you see twenty-five acres for sale locally, do you automatically think, I wonder where I could borrow another £250,000 to buy that?

Is your answer to low milk prices to milk more cows?

Is your answer to static milk prices to milk more cows?

Is your answer to high milk prices to milk more cows?

The average milk price at the moment is less than it was twenty years ago. Do you still believe it will turn around next year?

If the answer to any or all of the above is yes and you feel you may have a problem, you can look for help at www. DairyfarmersAnonymous.com.

If the website reminds you of displaced abomasums, then you really have problems and should get in touch as soon as possible.

88 April 2016

As I write this, Arla milk producers in Cornwall have just received news of another .75 p/litre cut in their milk price. The milk price is diabolical, with, as far as anyone can see, no likelihood of the price going up in the foreseeable future. Many dairy farmers will be trading at a loss and wondering whether there is any future for them milking cows for a living. This continuous cycle of boom and bust is no good to anyone, but I cannot see any answers. The Milk Marketing Board had its faults, but at least every milk producer was producing milk on a level playing field, unlike at the moment, where some producers are receiving 30 p/litre and others under 20 p/litre. A ludicrous situation.

By the time you read this, the situation may have resolved itself. Milk may be scarce, due to a drought in New Zealand or floods in America. The price may be back up to the mid 30s, or it may be down to under 20p.

I would just like to say to anyone contemplating selling their cows, that there is life after dairy farming. It may even be a better life. It took me nearly five years to get used to the idea and I hope this book has shown you part of the journey it has been.

Would I start dairy farming again?

I would rather stick pins in my eyes. However, if my son David came to me and said he really wanted to start milking again, we might look at it. My mother did not stand in my way when I tried to move farms fifteen years ago, and I would do my best not to stand in David's way. I would certainly not start milking at Witham again. It still has the same problems: hills, land locked and too small.

Glossary

Cornish and farming words that may be unfamiliar to some readers.

Arish – corn arish, stubble left in the field after the cereal crop has been combined.

Arish – Silage arish, stubble left in the field after the grass crop has been removed.

Bitch – Female of any species who is especially awkward and uncooperative.

Breaking in – Removing scrub and small trees from a field to allow it to be cropped.

Bullock –Young male beef animal.

Cattle Crush – cage for holding an animal securely while allowing the farmer or the vet to treat the animal safely.

Croust – mid morning snack, also referred to as crib.

Droke – small ditch or channel. A 'builders bum' can also be referred to as a droke.

Dung – organic manure that is straw based and can be piled.

Eavil – Four pronged, hand held fork used for moving dung. (see above).

Hedge – Hedgerow

Heifer – Female bovine up to the time that they calve for the second time, when they become a cow.

Rotavator – Machine for chopping the top two inches of soil to make it easier for the plough to bury all the trash.

Shit – Colloquial term given to all organic manure.

Glossary

Shit – Vulgarism or minor swear word.

Shit – Trouble, as in 'in the shit'.

Slurry – Organic manure that is liquid.

Urge – Retch

Wisht – Anything that is looking very poorly or unproductive.